Conscience and Prayer

Conscience and Prayer

The Spirit of Catholic Moral Theology

Dennis J. Billy, C.Ss.R.

James Keating

Preface by
Mark O'Keefe, O.S.B.

A Michael Glazier Book

THE LITURGICAL PRESS
Collegeville, Minnesota

www.litpress.org

A Michael Glazier Book published by The Liturgical Press

Cover design by David Manahan, O.S.B. Photo courtesty of PHOTOALTO.

1   2   3   4   5   6   7   8   9

Library of Congress Cataloging-in-Publication Data

Billy, Dennis Joseph.
    Conscience and prayer : the spirit of Catholic moral theology / Dennis J.
Billy, James F. Keating.
        p.   cm.
    "A Michael Glazier book."
    Includes bibliographical references and index.
    ISBN 0-8146-5957-8 (alk. paper)
    1. Prayer—Catholic Church.   2. Conscience—Religious aspects—Catholic
Church.   3. Christian ethics—Catholic authors.   4. Catholic Church—Doc-
trines.   I. Keating, James.   II. Title.

BJ1278.C66 B45 2002
241'.1—dc21

                                                                2001033745

We Dedicate this Book to Our Students;
Past, Present and Future
at both
The Alphonsian Academy in Rome
and
The Pontifical College Josephinum in Columbus

Contents

Preface

Prayer and conscience: It would be difficult to identify two more foundational elements of the moral life and of the spiritual life. The Second Vatican Council described the conscience as "the most secret core and sanctuary" of the human person where one "is alone with God, whose voice echoes in [one's] depths." It is therefore at the heart of the moral life, and its proper formation and functioning are essential to good moral decisions and to the development of a virtuous moral character. Prayer, as a "listening to" or "conversing with" or "communing with" God, is at the heart of any developing Christian spirituality. The authentic spiritual life of a Christian requires a commitment of prayer. Conscience and prayer: Both are foundational; both involve relationship with God; both fundamentally involve and require a listening to God.

Dennis Billy and James Keating, in their individual publications and in their previous collaborations, have already been major contributors to the current effort to bring together the academic disciplines of ethics and spirituality. By focusing their attention on conscience and prayer, they both advance the previous discussion and move it to a deeper level of reflection.

Implicit in their work, beyond their valuable service to the academic study of the moral and spiritual life of Christians, Billy and Keating point to the tremendous challenge that the meeting of spirituality and ethics issues to religious educators, preachers, liturgists and sacramental presiders, spiritual directors and parents. The already daunting challenges of forming consciences and of nurturing prayer are seen as necessarily related to one another. Having been convinced by their reflections, no longer can we hope properly to form the one without forming the other. At the same time, however, the challenge provides its own comfort: the formation of each promotes the authentic shaping of the other.

But the challenge issued by these reflections on conscience and prayer is not only a challenge to individuals or groups within the Church; it is a challenge to the entire Christian community. It is the challenge of the holistic formation of Christian disciples who are committed to seeking the holiness that requires not only prayer but also deeply formed Christian consciences.

The danger of the moral theology taught before the Second Vatican Council was that it promoted a minimalism for the "masses" of average Christians: obey the commandments and avoid sin. Spiritual theology and serious hope for holiness seemed reserved to an elite.

The danger of a renewed moral theology intimately linked with spirituality is not the danger that it will reduce the moral life to minimums, the "bottom-line" for luke-warm Christians. The danger, rather, is that it will promote a moral vision that seems too "lofty" for the many Christians who would think of "sanctity" as an unrealistic goal for their ordinary lives. In fact, of course, the Catholic vision of Church is wide and inclusive. The goal of forming morally good Christians must embrace men and women of various levels of commitment and stages of formation. But how to do both: to hold out the exalted vocation of Christians and, at the same time, make it seem attainable to the broad and varied community that calls itself Christian and Catholic?

The answer is not in seeking a moral theology of the lowest common denominator. The challenge is for the Church to take up whole-heartedly its evangelizing mission—the "new evangelization," as Pope John Paul II has called it—reaching out not only to those outside the Church but also calling Christians to a deeper, ongoing conversion of their lives. The challenge is the hard work of forming Christians who recognize the goal of holiness as the truest goal for their lives and who embrace the moral life as the authentic path to the communion with God which they long to know. It is a daunting task—a task requiring creativity, commitment, and constant appeal for the divine assistance.

Carrying forward the contemporary discussion of the essential relationship of ethics and spirituality, of our moral and spiritual lives, Dennis Billy and James Keating have made clearer the awesome challenge for the Church and for those who teach, form, guide, preach, direct and lead others within the Church. But accepting anew the Good News of Jesus Christ leads necessarily to the response which is both good moral living and prayer. Men and women who recognize the divine love for sinners respond by striving to conform their lives to that love in their daily decisions and relationships and by seeking to draw near to the love that calls them into communion.

By their careful and insightful reflection on the relationship of prayer and conscience in the Christian life, Billy and Keating have both pointed to the fundamental evangelizing mission of the Church and provided fresh insight into the authentic foundation in conscience and prayer from which Christian men and women can respond to the Good News in their lives.

Moral theologians, our authors remind us, must want to be saints. Dennis Billy and James Keating show us in this present book that moral theologians must also be disciples who ask how the Church can help other men and women to hear, embrace, and live the call to sanctity in their lives.

Mark O'Keefe, O.S.B.
President-Rector, St. Meinrad School of Theology, Indiana
Professor of Moral Theology

Introduction

This book evolved out of our common interest in exploring the relationship between spirituality and morality in the Roman Catholic tradition. The connection between these two very important areas of theological inquiry is the subject of much current interest. This development is due, at least in part, to the heightened popular interest in spirituality itself and the attempt by scholars to understand its impact on all areas of human existence—including that of morality.

Unfortunately, much of what has been written to date on this topic concerns only the general contours of the relationship and has not investigated in great detail the impact that some of the most fundamental categories of these disciplines have on one another. Our examination of the relationship between prayer and conscience in the Roman Catholic tradition represents an initial attempt to address this concern. Through it, we hope to open up new areas of research into the nature of the Catholic spiritual moral life and to carry the discussion about the relationship between spirituality and morality to an even deeper level.

We have divided the book into five chapters. Chapter One, "The Reciprocity of Prayer and Conscience," looks at the meaning of the terms and examines their historical interaction. Chapter Two, "Spirit and Reason," provides the anthropological foundations for "reason's spiritual rebirth" and discusses the role of prayer in Catholic moral theological reflection. Chapter Three, "Listening, Prayer, and Conscience Formation," presents "rapt listening" as the way prudence manifests itself in the spiritual moral lives of believers. Chapter Four, "Prayer and Conscience: Openness to the Truth of Christ," examines some of the key elements involved in what has typically been referred to as "putting on the mind of Christ." Chapter Five, "Jesus as the Norm of the Spiritual Moral Life," looks at the practical implications of what listening to Christ and his body in prayer means for conscience formation. In our conclusion, we provide a succinct statement of how an integrated understanding of prayer and conscience represents a middle way that will help Christian ethical reflection steer clear of the extremes of rationalism and fideism.

It bears noting that parts of Chapter Two have already been published by one of us as "A 'Spiritual Turn' for Catholic Moral Theology," *Review for Religious* 57 (1998) 595–604, and "Christ's Redemptive Journey and the Moral Dimensions of Prayer," *Studia moralia* 37 (1999) 127–51. We wish to thank the publishers of these journals for granting us permission to reprint parts of these articles in a slightly different form.

Dennis J. Billy, C.Ss.R.
James Keating

Chapter One

The Reciprocity of Prayer and Conscience:
Historical Considerations

"A good conscience is found through prayer, and pure prayer through conscience. Each by nature needs the other."[1] This observation from *The Philokalia,* an anthology of spiritual texts from Eastern Orthodoxy, reminds us of the close, reciprocal relationship that spirituality and morality can share in the daily lives of believing Christians. Holiness and goodness are not unrelated spheres of human experience, but two sides of the same existential coin. Prayer helps conscience by opening it up to the divine and enabling it to discern more clearly the good to be done and the evil to be avoided in the daily circumstances of life. Conscience, in turn, helps prayer by providing the moral starting point from which a person sets out and seeks with each new day to love more intensely and walk more closely with the Lord. Each needs, and can hardly do without, the other. They are the two legs with which Christians set out each day to walk together with Christ in their journey to God.

In this chapter, we will examine the historical contours of this reciprocal relationship between prayer and conscience. We will do so in a simple and straightforward manner. After taking a look at the meaning of the terms themselves and, in the case of conscience, the historical development of the concept, we will examine their interplay at various moments of the Church's history, and conclude with some brief

[1] *The Philokalia: The Complete Text,* trans. G.E.H. Palmer, Philip Sherrard, Kallistos Ware, vol. 1 (Boston: Faber and Faber, 1979) 123.

1

qualifying observations about their interaction within the Christian community. Our goal here is to paint in broad, colorful strokes a general picture of how this relationship was understood in the past so that we can get a better sense of the Church's present spiritual moral horizons.

What is Prayer?

There have been so many volumes written about the nature of Christian prayer that it may seem presumptuous for us to try to treat it in such summary fashion. Much can be said, however, for going directly to the heart of prayer and for treating it in a clear and succinct manner. The Scriptures promote a very simple teaching. In the Lord's prayer, Jesus teaches us to pray with childlike trust to God (Matt 6:10-13). He calls God, "Abba, Father" (Mark 14:36) and enjoins us to bring all our needs to God: "Ask, and it will be given you; seek, and you will find; knock, and it will be opened to you" (Matt 7:7).[2] He bids us to trust that God has our best interests at heart: "What father among you, if his son asks for a fish, will instead of a fish give him a serpent?" (Luke 11:11). In the Epistles, Paul reminds the Church at Rome that it is because of a spirit of adoption that they cry out "Abba, Father" (Rom 8:15) and the Spirit helps them in their weakness ". . . with sighs too deep for words" (Rom 8:26). His injunction "to pray constantly" (1Thess 5:17), moreover, extends to the entire Church at Thessalonica, not to a select, proficient few.

Christianity proposes that *everyone* has an open invitation to pray to God and to share an intimate relationship with God. Manuals of spiritual theology have traditionally gotten this point across by stating that everyone receives sufficient grace to pray. Responding to that grace is another matter altogether; some of us do, some of us do not. The choice is ours to make, and our destiny depends on it. Prayer has been called "the great means of salvation."[3] It helps us to put all that happens to us in perspective and promises to effect in us an intimate participation in the life of God. Christ, the *Logos*, makes it possible. Eternally generated from the Father and born of a woman, the Word of God now wishes to be born in our hearts. This Word wants to dwell within us so that we

---

[2] The English translations of all New Testament texts come from the Revised Standard Version (2nd ed., 1971) as found in Nestle-Aland, *Greek-English New Testament*, 3rd ed. (Stuttgart: Deutsche Bibelgesellschaft, 1986).

[3] Alphonsus de Liguori, Saint, *The Great Means of Salvation and of Perfection*, ed. Eugene Grimm, *The Complete Works of Saint Alphonsus de Liguori*, vol. 3 (Brooklyn: Redemptorist Fathers, 1927) 19.

might dwell in God. "Paradise for God is the human heart." These words from Alphonsus Liguori's, *On Conversing Continually and Familiarly with God* (1754),[4] remind us that Jesus, who is "Emmanuel," i.e., God with us (Isa 7:14), yearns for his Spirit to dwell within our hearts. Through prayer, God actively works in our lives to make God's deepest dreams for us come true.

There are many definitions of prayer. For John Damascene (c. 675–c. 749), it is ". . . the raising of one's mind and heart to God or the requesting of good things from God."[5] For Thérèse of Lisieux (1873–1897), it is ". . . a surge of the heart . . . a simple look turned toward heaven . . . a cry of recognition and of love, embracing both trial and joy."[6] The Curé of Ars (1786–1859) tells the story of a peasant describing it as a simple gaze of faith.[7] *The Catechism of the Catholic Church* uses the categories of gift, covenant, and communion to ascertain its nature.[8] According to some ancient sources, prayer is nothing more than "keeping company with God."[9] This last definition may very well be the simplest (and most profound) of all. Just as there are many ways of "being present to" or "keeping company with" another person (e.g., sharing a meal, writing a letter, talking on the phone), so too there are analogous ways in which a person can place him or herself in the presence of God. The traditional threefold division of vocal prayer *(oratio)*, mental prayer *(meditatio)*, and contemplation *(contemplatio)* verifies this claim, as does the classification of prayer into various types (e.g., adoration, petition, intercession, thanksgiving), and the many prayer forms that have been developed over the years to help us deepen our relationship with God. Time and space do not permit us to examine the historical development of the various prayer forms in the Christian tradition. It is important for us to remember, however, that the history of *how* people pray (liturgically or otherwise) says a great deal about their understanding of God, themselves, and the world they live in. It also will have an impact on their understanding of the relationship between the spiritual and moral spheres of their lives and the way they view the

---

[4] Alphonsus de Liguori, *The Way of Salvation and of Perfection*, ed. Eugene Grimm, *The Complete Works of Saint Alphonsus de Liguori*, vol. 2 (Brooklyn: Redemptorist Fathers, 1926) 395.

[5] Catholic Church, *Catechism of the Catholic Church* (Vatican City: Libreria Editrice Vaticana, 1994) 2559. Hereafter referred to as *CCC* and referenced by paragraph numbers.

[6] *CCC*, Preface to 2559.

[7] *CCC* 2715.

[8] *CCC* 2559–65.

[9] Clement of Alexandria, *Stromata* 7:7 (PG 9:455); Evagrius Ponticus, *De oratione* 3 (PG 79.1167). Cited in Simon Tugwell, *Prayer*, vol. 1 (Dublin: Veritas Publications, 1974) vii.

relationship between prayer and conscience. To offset this unfortunate lacuna in our present discussion, pertinent historical examples about changing perceptions and patterns of Christian prayer will be brought in at appropriate times as the chapter unfolds.

"Truly, I say to you, whoever does not receive the kingdom of God like a little child shall not enter it (Mark 10:15)." When all is said and done, prayer is nothing more than a simple, childlike conversation with God. It can be done in the privacy of one's room or in a communal setting. It reaches its height at the liturgy, when the Church with Christ at its head prays to God in the Spirit. As with any authentic conversation, prayer involves *speaking* (with the voice, with the mind, with the heart) and *listening*. Since Jesus asks us to love God with all our heart, soul, and strength (Luke 10:27), it follows that prayer, one of the deepest signs of an individual's love for God, must also involve *every* dimension of human existence, the physical, emotional, mental, spiritual, and social (Cf. 1 Thess 5:23, Eph 1:23, Col 1:18). We need, in other words, to find ways of talking and listening to God with our bodies, our feelings, our thoughts, our spirits, and with others. We also need to talk and listen to God in and through our relationship to the world, which sustains us and enables us to live in human society. Much of the struggle we encounter in the spiritual life involves finding the particular rhythm that incorporates these various dimensions of prayer into our lives in appropriate and suitable ways.[10] For our present purposes, it is important to note that conscience has traditionally been thought of in Catholic circles as a universal dimension of human existence. As such, it too can and should be opened up to God in prayer. To understand just what this might entail, however, it is important for us to have a clear understanding of its nature and scope.

What is Conscience?

As with prayer, the volumes upon volumes that have been written on conscience make one wonder what contribution a merely cursory treatment of it could possibly make. A brief summary of its historical development in the Christian tradition, however, can be helpful for a variety of reasons. For one thing, it will help us to draw a distinction between conscience itself and the language used to describe it. For another, it will serve to show that a variety of understandings of con-

---

[10] See Dennis J. Billy, *Evangelical Kernels: A Theological Spirituality of the Religious Life* (Staten Island, N.Y.: Alba House, 1993) 167–84, esp. 170–73; Fabio Giardini, *Pray without Ceasing: Toward a Systematic Psychotheology of Christian Prayerlife* (Rome: Millennium/Gracewing, 1998) 15–37, 299–301.

science have arisen in the Christian tradition (some more popular than others). For yet another, it will serve to underscore the various levels at which it functions and highlight the importance of developing resources for a sound formation of conscience within the Christian community.

Our word "conscience" comes from the Latin word "conscientia" meaning "a joint knowledge" or "knowledge with." It has traditionally been understood in the psychological sense of "consciousness" and in the strictly moral sense of "a consciousness of right and wrong." *Syneidesis*, its Greek equivalent, conveys these two senses, as well as the broader moral connotation of "conscientiousness." It appears in the Greek New Testament, especially in the letters of St. Paul, who employs it in all three senses, but with a special predilection for the second.[11]

The term *syneidesis* achieved even more prominence in early Christian vocabulary when St. Jerome (c. 347–419/20) used it in an allegorical interpretation of Ezekiel's vision of the four living creatures, each with faces of a human, a lion, a bull, and an eagle (Ezek 1:4-28). After citing the well-known interpretation that associated these faces with the four evangelists, he remarks that the more common interpretation is to understand them as a symbolic rendering of the Platonic understanding of the soul. According to this interpretation, the faces of the human, the lion, and the bull correspond to the rational, irascible, and concupiscible powers of the soul. Influenced by the allegorical exegesis of Origen (c. 185–c. 253/4), who in a homily on the passage adapts the typical Platonic view of the soul from a threefold to a fourfold dynamism, Jerome identifies the eagle with "the spark of conscience" *(scintilla conscientiae)* which hovers over the other rational, irascible, and concupiscible powers and corrects them when they err. According to Jerome, the Greeks referred to this "spark of conscience" as *syneidesis* and often identified it with the human spirit. Although Origen never actually makes this identification in his homily, he does so explicitly in his commentary on Romans 2:14-15.[12]

The history of the term becomes even more complicated when, sometime before the twelfth century, a copyist of Jerome's commentary

---

[11] For an expanded treatment, see: *A Latin Dictionary: Founded on Andrews' Edition of Freund's Latin Dictionary*, eds. Charlton T. Lewis and Charles Short (Oxford: Clarendon Press, 1879; 1980 impression), s.v. "conscientia." *A Greek-English Lexicon of the New Testament and Other Early Christian Literature*, ed. Walter Bauer, trans. William F. Arndt and F. Wilber Gingrich, revised and adapted by F. Wilber Gingrich and Frederick W. Danker (Chicago: The University of Chicago Press, 1958; 2nd ed., 1979), s.v. "syneidesis."

[12] See Jerome, *Commentarium in Ezechielem* 1.1 (PL 25.22). For a text critical study of Jerome's text that corrects the errors of the Migne edition, see Jacques de Blick, "Syndérèse ou conscience," *Revue d'ascètique et de mystique* 75 (1949) 146–57. For the relevant texts from Origen, see below n. 25.

on Ezekiel mistakenly writes the word *synteresis* instead of *syneidesis*. This distinction was passed down through Rabanus Maurus (d. 856) through Peter Lombard (c. 1100–c. 1160/5) to Master Udo (d. after 1165), who was the first to specifically identify this new word with "the spark of reason *(scintilla rationis)*." In their respect for the authority of tradition and their love for clarity, scholastic theologians such as Phillip the Chancellor (c. 1160/85–1236), Alexander of Hales (1186–1245), Albert the Great (1200–1280), and others developed a variety of imaginative and highly original theories to differentiate *synderesis* from conscience.[13]

Two of the more comprehensive proposals came from Bonaventure of Bagnoregio (c. 1217–1274) and Thomas Aquinas (1224/5–1274). Bonaventure, the representative par excellence of the Franciscan school, identifies *synderesis* as a "dispositional potency" of the will that naturally directs it toward the good. He also uses a hybrid version of Augustinian illuminationism and Aristotelian abstractionism to create a two-tiered notion of conscience. The first is both an innate and acquired habit of the practical reason that is incapable of error and that gives us certain knowledge of the primary principles of the natural law (e.g., "do good and avoid evil"). The second is an entirely acquired habit of the practical reason that is capable of error and that seeks to determine the moral good through a process of deliberation. Thomas, the representative par excellence of the Dominican school, relies more heavily on Aristotle in his formulation of the nature of moral cognition. He identifies *synderesis* as a natural habit of practical reason that contains the primary principles of the natural law (e.g., "do and pursue the good; avoid evil"). Once supplied with the necessary data from sense perception, it also provides self-evident knowledge of the basic human goods and of an individual's need to live a virtuous life. Conscience, by way of contrast, is a judgment of the practical reason that forms the conclusion of a practical syllogism. Since the will is naturally oriented toward the good presented to it by reason, he sees no need for it to have a special habit or dispositional power to help it along.[14]

The richness and quality of the scholastic discussion on *synderesis* and conscience leads one to conclude that medieval theologians would probably have developed a multilevel understanding of moral cogni-

[13] For an expanded history of the term, see R. C. Petzäl, "Conscience ou syndérèse: De l'aigle d'Ezéchiel à la conscience morale par le commentaire de St. Jerome," *Theoria* 20 (1954) 64–77; M. B. Crowe, "The Term *Synderesis* and the Scholastics," *Irish Theological Quarterly* 23 (1956) 151–64, 228–45.

[14] For an extended comparison of Bonaventure and Aquinas on conscience, see Dennis J. Billy, "The Authority of Conscience in Bonaventure and Aquinas," *Studia Moralia* 31 (1993) 237–63.

tion on their own, even if the scribal error had never occurred. For our present purposes, it is important to point out that this discussion produced a variety of understandings of the nature of conscience and the way it functioned. Bonaventure and Aquinas, for example, held very different views on the authority of an erroneous conscience. For the former, a person is obliged to change it; for the latter, a person is bound to it as long as it endures. They also used a very different nomenclature for explaining their ideas and supported their claims with competing theories of knowledge.

This vitality of opinions continued in the subtle distinctions Duns Scotus (c. 1266–1308), a Franciscan friar whose mitigated moral voluntarism highlighted the love of God in the Christian spiritual moral life and represented a middle position between Aquinas' rational philosophical position on the immutability of certain basic moral principles and the Franciscan nominalist, William of Ockham (c. 1285–c. 1347), for whom the entire moral law depended entirely on the arbitrary decision of God. This voluntaristic turn of Scotus actually paved the way for Ockham and his unrelenting application of his principle of parsimony (i.e., "Ockham's razor"), a development which undercut all previous theological syntheses and which had a drastic effect on the moral and spiritual life of late medieval Western Christianity. Nominalism denies the existence of universals (of either the Platonic or the Aristotelian type) and only allows for the existence of particulars. Universals are names created by the human mind and cannot reveal the true nature of reality. The result is the inability to argue rationally to the existence of God or the existence of a stable natural order. God's will and God's will alone is responsible for the order perceived in the universe—and even *it* is subject to change. Ockham *does* draw the distinction, however, between God's absolute power *(potentia absoluta)* and God's ordered power *(potentia ordinata)*. While the former emphasizes God's radical freedom to change any element of the created order (including the moral law), the latter recognizes the way he actually operates in creation. For Ockham, "right reason" and "conscience" are a part of God's ordained power and allowed for the possibility of a natural law ethics. For him, leading a moral life means following the judgments of "right reason" and obeying the commands of divine revelation, while also acknowledging God's radical freedom to permit what is forbidden. In this way, obedience to God's will takes qualified precedence over the judgment of conscience. In any given instance, one always has to admit at least the possibility of a change in the divine will.[15]

[15] For the interdependence of Scotus' and Ockham's ideas, see Gordon Leff, *The Dissolution of the Medieval Outlook: An Essay on the Intellectual and Spiritual Change in*

The extreme emphasis on obedience to authority in late medieval thought paved the way for Reformation and Counter-Reformation, a split in the religious psyche of Western Christianity that even to this day remains deep and in urgent need of healing. Prior to this scandalous break, a more conciliatory effort at reform came from the insights of Christian humanism, the most eloquent spokesman of which was Erasmus of Rotterdam (1469–1536), a Renaissance man who played a vital role in restoring the Greek New Testament to the Western Church. Erasmus and Christian humanists like him reacted against the narrow scholasticism of the late medieval period by taking a critical look at the sources of Christianity and by enshrining the classical texts of ancient Greece and Rome. They emphasized the basic dignity and goodness of the human person, the ability of that person to exercise free will in a way that would contribute to his or her salvation, and the importance of a detailed daily examination of conscience. Their understanding of the latter concept was mutually influenced by their critical study of the sources of both Christianity and Greco-Roman civilization. They represented a critical, yet calm, mediating voice in an age of growing religious antagonisms, one that produced profound scholarly insights into the tradition but whose gradual and measured strategy for reform would go unheeded.[16]

It would be impossible in this brief survey to include the great variety of positions on conscience of the conservative and radical reformed moralities, exemplified by such diverse figures as Martin Luther (1483–1546), for the conservative reformers, and John Calvin (1509–1564) and Ulrich Zwingli (1484–1531) for the radical reformers. For our present purposes, it suffices to say that both streams of the reform movement were influenced by and reacted against the very nominalist positions that had heralded in the breakdown of the medieval synthesis. On the one hand, they agreed with the need for revelation because of their be-

---

the Fourteenth Century (New York: Harper & Row, 1976) 32–92, esp. 54–57. For Scotus' moral method, see Thomas A. Shannon, "Method in Ethics: A Scotistic Contribution," *The Context of Casuistry,* eds. James F. Keenan and Thomas A. Shannon (Washington, D.C.: Georgetown, 1995), 3–24. For moral obligation in William of Ockham, see Louis Vereecke, *De Guillaume d'Ockham à Saint Alphonse de Liguori: Etudes d'histoire de la théologie morale moderne 1300-1787, Bibliotheca historica Congregationis Ssmi Redemptoris,* vol. 12 (Rome: Collegium S. Alfonsi de Urbe, 1986) 149–67; Lucan Freppert, *The Basis of Morality According to William Ockham* (Chicago: Franciscan Herald Press, 1988) 83–140.

[16] See Walter J. Woods, *Walking with Faith: New Perspectives on the Sources and Shaping of Catholic Moral Life* (Collegeville, Minn.: The Liturgical Press, 1998) 363–65. See also William Manchester, *A World Lit Only by Fire: The Medieval Mind and the Renaissance: Portrait of an Age* (Boston: Little, Brown and Company, 1992) 117–27, 180–89.

lief in humanity's radical corruption by Original Sin and its resulting incapacity to justify itself before God. On the other hand, they were repulsed by what was to them an undue emphasis on obedience to the law and the ordained authority (e.g., the Catholic hierarchy). No law, wherever it came from, had the power to save. The reformers also reacted against the exaltation of the human by the Renaissance and Christian humanist return to the sources of the so-called Golden Age of Greek and Roman civilization. They pledged their allegiance to the Gospel alone that, through the gifts of grace and faith in Christ, justified them in spite of their sin as sons and daughters of God. Within this larger theological framework, conscience generally came to be understood as an appeal to inner experience manifesting itself in: (1) an intellectual element that sought to *know* the will of God through reason or "the inner light of the Spirit" and (2) an element of conscious, dynamic striving that looked to the influence of grace, conversion, and sanctification in order to *do* the will of God. This intellectual appeal to conscience was often supplemented by an appeal to an inward divine experience, made possible by a living faith and the illuminating gifts of the Holy Spirit.[17]

The Catholic response to the Reformation was comprehensive and far-reaching. The council fathers of Trent used Thomistic categories to clarify their position on the most hotly debated issues (e.g., revelation, Original Sin, justification and grace, the priesthood). Through the teaching and example of a series of very remarkable saints (e.g., Ignatius of Loyola [1491–1556], Teresa of Avila [1515–1582], John of the Cross [1542–1591]) they also promoted a variety of kataphatic and apophatic mysticisms to attract the faithful to their institutional reforms. The latter was highly successful, for it shored up the Catholic identity in an area that was particularly vulnerable to the criticism of the reformers. It continues to this day to attract believers of various backgrounds to the Catholic tradition within which these spiritualities were first conceived and fostered. The former had the dual effect of enshrining Aquinas as the philosopher and theologian par excellence of the Catholic Church and of refocusing the efforts of Catholic theology away from the nominalist concerns that had occupied it during the previous two centuries. Thomas, however, was read selectively when used as an instrument to defend the faith against the arguments of the Reformers. The result was often a truncated Thomism that failed to

---

[17] See R.E.O. White, *The Insights of History,* The Changing Continuity of Christian Ethics Ser. 2 (Exeter, England: The Paternoster Press, 1981) 225–26, 241. For the general contours of Protestant ethics, see Servais Pinckaers, *The Sources of Christian Ethics,* trans. Mary Thomas Noble (3rd ed.; Edinburgh: T. & T. Clark, 1995) 282–86.

capture the inquisitive spirit of his method and the true height and depth and breadth of his learning. Because this brand of Thomism was guided by the questions the Counter-Reformers were seeking to address, it follows that it too was influenced, at least peripherally, by the concerns of law and authority promulgated by late medieval nominalism.[18]

From the Council of Trent onwards, Thomas would hold a privileged place in Catholic theology. Since that time, there have been a number of intellectual movements dedicated to his thought, all of which have had an important impact on the understanding and presentation of the Catholic position on conscience.[19] In addition to having to deal with the criticisms of the Protestant Reformers, the Catholic Church also had to steer a middle course in the seventeenth and early eighteenth centuries between the dangerous extremes of Jansenist rigorism, which placed heavy ascetical demands upon its adherents, and moral laxism, which recognized virtually no restraints whatsoever. It did so by developing a manualist tradition of moral casuistry, which developed various means of resolving doubts of conscience before the law (e.g., probabilism, probabiliorism, equiprobabilism). For the proponents of moral casuistry, conscience was nearly always understood in the narrow sense of a particular judgment about the moral goodness of an act. Moral theology during this period was closely associated with the jurisprudence of both civil and canon law and it was not uncommon for its practitioners, like Alphonsus Liguori (1696–1787), the founder of the Redemptorists and the champion of the equiprobabilist position, to be trained in both.[20]

Overlapping this period and extending well into later centuries, the Church confronted questions arising from the Enlightenment and the dispersion of secular humanism. Basing themselves on the nominalist rejection of universals and the Cartesian concern for "clear and distinct" ideas, the proponents of the Enlightenment developed the basic criteria for scientific observation and empirical research. This thirst for

---

[18] For the influence of nominalism on both Protestant and Counter Reformational ethics, see Pinckaers, *The Sources of Christian Ethics*, 290–92.

[19] See Thomas F. O'Meara, *Thomas Aquinas: Theologian* (Notre Dame, Ind.: University of Notre Dame Press, 1997) 152–200; Gerald McCool, *From Unity to Pluralism: The Internal Evolution of Thomism* (New York: Fordham University Press, 1992).

[20] For the emergence of the manual tradition, see Pinckaers, *The Sources of Christian Ethics*, 254–79; John A. Gallagher, *Time Past, Time Future: An Historical Study of Catholic Moral Theology* (Mahwah, N.J.: Paulist Press, 1990) 29–47. For the moral system of St. Alphonsus, see Théodule Rey-Mermet, *Moral Choices: The Moral Theology of Saint Alphonsus Liguori*, trans. Paul Laverdure (Liguori, Mo.: Liguori Publications, 1998) 67–89; Vereecke, *De Guillaume d'Ockham à Saint Alphonse de Liguori*, 551–66.

inductive reasoning and verifying empirical data spilled over into other intellectual disciplines and was largely responsible for such momentous developments as the rise of deism, an increasingly mechanized view of the universe, the growing separation of the sacred and secular sphere of Western society, and the formulation of the basic criteria of the historical-critical method. For centuries, the Catholic Church's approach to the Enlightenment and secular humanism was to adopt a reactive, "fortress" mentality through which it sought to shelter the Catholic faithful from what it considered the unhealthy dangers of the modernist outlook.[21]

The manualist tradition of Catholic moral theology remained an integral part of this closed-in, insular outlook from the seventeenth right up to the end of the first half of the twentieth century—and, to a large extent, even beyond. Not even the so-called masters of suspicion (Marx, Nietzsche and Freud), whose ground-breaking insights detected previously unnoticed cracks in the commonly accepted vision of modernity (and thus paved the way for its gradual dissolution), could mitigate its claims on the Catholic mindset. Although voices of reform within the Church were heard with increasing frequency, real change only came when the precipitous events of the Second World War rang the death knoll for the naive optimism of the modern world and a series of powerful scientific, economic, and cultural changes heralded in the dawn of the postmodern era. The Catholic Church reacted to the rapid changes of the second half of the twentieth century, cautiously at first, but then with a call for a spirit of *aggiornamento* at the Second Vatican Council that would open it up to dialogue with the world. Part of that renewal took place in attempts by moral theologians to root their thinking in Gospel values and around the person of Jesus Christ. In addition to being examined in the context of the Hebrew notion of "heart" and the use of *syneidesis* in the Pauline corpus and other New Testament texts, conscience was examined from a variety of philosophical vantage points such as personalism, phenomenology, and a more historically sensitive understanding of Thomistic texts. Theologians also used the insights of analytical and developmental psychology to distinguish conscience from the superego and to show how it changes during a person's life and can be classified into clearly defined developmental stages. They also have used the concept to examine the possibility of an autonomous ethics and to examine, with varying degrees of success, such sensitive issues as dissent against Church teaching, arguments

---

[21] See Dennis J. Billy, "The Unfolding of a Tradition," *Spirituality and Morality: Integrating Prayer and Action,* eds. Dennis J. Billy and Donna Lynn Orsuto (Mahwah, N.J.: Paulist Press, 1996) 22–24. See also Woods, *Walking with Faith* 468–81.

from proportionalism, and the meaning and viability of the fundamental option. The result has been a much broader (and deeper) understanding of the term that addressed every dimension of human existence, while at the same time remaining true to the rigors of theological inquiry. Many Catholic theologians today accept a threefold understanding of conscience as (1) a capacity, (2) a process, and (3) a judgment—what Thomas would respectively associate with *synderesis*, the process of deliberation, and the judgment of conscience itself. They also are keen to point out the communal dimension of conscience formation, stating that only a genuine "reciprocity of consciences" can promote the health and development of an individual conscience. Recent magisterial documents, in addition to being rooted in Scripture and showing a marked sensitivity to the complexity of the current understanding of the term, show a clear preference for the clarity and precision of the traditional Thomistic categories and terminology.[22]

The Relationship Between Prayer and Conscience

This historical overview reminds us that conscience is a single word with myriad connotations. One cannot simply assume that, at any given time, it has the same meaning for all Christian writers (Bonaventure and Aquinas being cases in point). To understand what a particular author means by it, one must examine the text in its historical context and take into account the various factors influencing it (e.g.,

[22] Some of the better known theological presentations of conscience appear in Richard M. Gula, *Reason Informed by Faith: Foundations of Catholic Morality* (Mahwah, N.J.: Paulist Press, 1989) 123–35; Timothy E. O'Connell, *Principles for a Catholic Morality* (San Francisco: Harper & Row, 1978) 83–97; Bernard Häring, "Conscience: The Sanctuary of Creative Fidelity and Liberty," *Introduction to Christian Ethics: A Reader*, eds. Ronald P. Hamel and Kenneth R. Himes (Mahwah, N.J.: Paulist Press, 1989) 252–80. For a critique of some aspects of these approaches see David Matzko McCarthy, "Conscience: A Richer Moral Language" *Josephinum Journal of Theology* 8:1 (Winter/Spring 2001). Although the Church does not canonize any one philosophy [John Paul II, Pope, *Fides et Ratio* (Vatican City: Libreria Editrice Vaticana, 1998) 49], its preference for Thomistic categories and terminology comes through in many recent magisterial statements. For example, the presentation of the morality of a human act in *Catechism* (CCC 1749-56) is heavily Thomistic, as is much of the presentation in "Part Three: Life in Christ." The presentation of "natural law" in John Paul II's encyclical letter *Veritatis Splendor* [(Vatican City: Libreria Editrice Vaticana, 1993; 4th printing, 1996) 44] has strong Thomistic overtones, as does the presentation of conscience as "a practical judgment" [57–60]. See also the reference to "the enduring originality of the thought of Thomas Aquinas" and the necessity "to reiterate the Angelic Doctor's insights and insist on the study of his thought" in John Paul II's encyclical letter *Fides et Ratio* (43–44, 61).

psychological, anthropological, philosophical, theological, etc.). The same can be said for the way in which conscience is understood in its relationship to prayer. What follows is a broad overview of their interaction in the Christian tradition.

1. To begin with, it bears noting that the question we are posing probably would not have been counted as particularly relevant by the earliest generations of Christians. The deep sense of urgency with which this expanding "movement of converts" awaited the coming of the kingdom would have made them little concerned about the finer points of the interaction of the moral and spiritual spheres of their lives. Nor were these spheres considered distinct in the life of the Spirit that sustained their communities and gave direction both to the way they prayed and how they lived their lives. "Prayer" and "heart," two values deeply rooted in the Hebrew mentality spilled over naturally into the communities established by Jesus' earliest disciples. For these communities, it was the Spirit who moved the Church to open its heart to God in prayer. Prayer and conscience were two distinct yet closely related dimensions of the community's real participation in the life and mind of Christ, the transforming presence of whom revivified its members at baptism and communed with them in a tangible way in the breaking of the bread.[23]

2. It was only when the expectation of Christ's imminent return began to waver that serious thought was given to the deeper questions marking the historical sojourn of the Christian community. Christian missionaries proclaimed the Gospel in *Koiné* Greek and began to adapt Greek philosophical concepts to the exigencies of the Gospel proclamation. In his missionary journeys, Paul had already gone to great lengths to translate the Good News to the Greek-speaking peoples of the Mediterranean world. His frequent use of a term like *syneidesis* (with its various connotations) represents just one small example of an effort of translation and adaptation of Christianity to the Hellenic world. This process of inculturation had a deep impact on the thought patterns of the developing Church. It would extend beyond Paul's life to the Christian apologists of the second and third centuries, and eventually mark one of the great successes of the Church's missionary efforts. For centuries to come, the philosophical orientation of the Greek mind would invigorate Christian theology with new insights into the meaning

---

[23] For the relationship between early Christianity and conversion, as well as a treatment of the moral implications of baptism and Eucharist, see Wayne A. Meeks, *The Origins of Christian Morality: The First Two Centuries* (New Haven: Yale University Press, 1993) 18–36, 92–98. For the various virtues encouraged in early Christian communities, see Benjamin W. Farley, *In Praise of Virtue: An Exploration of the Biblical Virtues in a Cultural Context* (Grand Rapids, Mich.: Eerdmans, 1995) 95–157.

of the faith. The insights of Stoicism, and Middle Platonism, as well as the philosophical mysticism of Neoplatonism were used to penetrate the mystery of the Christ event and draw out its ramifications for Christian living.[24]

3. One of the more creative attempts at delineating the contours of the relationship between prayer and conscience comes from Origen, head of the catechetical school in Alexandria in the first part of the third century. As mentioned earlier, he changed the tripartite Platonic understanding of the soul to a fourfold dynamism and used it to make an allegorical interpretation of the four-faced creatures of Ezek 1:4-28. For him, spirit *(pneuma)* was the eagle which hovers *over* the rational, irascible, and concupiscible dimensions of the soul and prevents them from erring. Later, in his commentary on Rom 2:14-15 he explicitly identified the human spirit with conscience *(syneidesis)*. When seen in this light, Rom 8:16 reveals a very close relationship between prayer and conscience: ". . . the Spirit of God bears witness with our spirit (i.e., conscience) that we are children of God." It is in and through the human spirit (i.e., conscience) that the Holy Spirit communes with us and ". . . intercedes for us with sighs too deep for words" (Rom 8:26). For Origen, the human spirit is the supreme faculty of the soul which has the capacity to commune with the Spirit of God and, precisely for that reason, is capable of a certain co-knowledge (i.e., *conscientia*) with God. Here, prayer and conscience come together in the highest dimension of the human soul. One effects the union of the divine and human; the other directs the human toward the good and away from evil.[25]

4. It has already been mentioned how Jerome based his own interpretation of Ezek 1:4-28 on Origen's commentary and how, in time, errors in the manuscript tradition eventually led to the introduction of the new word *synteresis,* a development which ultimately led scholastic scholars of the twelfth, and especially the thirteenth, centuries to posit a two-tiered understanding of conscience. What has not been men-

---

[24] For Christianity's integration of Greco-Roman culture and for the stages of its assimilation of Greek philosophy, see Pinckaers, *The Sources of Christian Ethics,* 203–6. See also Jean Daniélou, *Gospel Message and Hellenistic Culture,* trans. John Austin Baker, A History of Early Christian Doctrine before the Council of Nicea Ser. 2, (Philadelphia: The Westminster Press, 1973) esp. 31–73, 303–22; W.H.C. Frend, *The Rise of Christianity* (Philadelphia: Fortress Press, 1984) esp. 367–95, 553–91.

[25] See Origen, *Homiliae in Ezechielem* 1.16 (PG 13.681); Origen, *Commentariorum in epistolas S. Pauli ad Romanos* 2.9 (PG 14.893, 1105–6, 1119–21). For Origen's allegorical approach to the Bible, see Robert M. Grant and David Tracy, *A Short History of the Interpretation of the Bible* (2nd ed.; Philadelphia: Fortress Press, 1984) 52–62. For the moral implications of his thought, see Robert L Wilken, "Alexandria: A School for Training in Virtue," *Schools of Thought in the Christian Tradition,* ed. Patrick Henry (Philadelphia: Fortress, 1984) 15–30.

tioned thus far is that the scholastic treatment of conscience in this period was interested in locating and then classifying humankind's naturally endowed powers of moral cognition, thereby relegating prayer to the periphery of the discussion. That is not to say that the scholastics denigrated prayer as a way of knowing the good or that they thought it irrelevant for leading a moral life. On the contrary, it would be difficult to find more zealous proponents of the centrality of prayer in the Christian moral life than Bonaventure and Aquinas. It only means that the scholastic love for classification demanded that prayer be treated (often at length) under a different heading. Bonaventure's spiritual treatises represent some of the finest treasures of the Church's mystical tradition. Thomas' presentation of prayer and devotion in his discussion of the interior acts of religion, an allied virtue of justice, can hardly be matched for its clarity and comprehensive scope. Nor can his treatment of the gifts of the Spirit as the culmination of the infused virtues. Scholastic theologians understood and respected the necessity of prayer for salvation and the living out of the moral life. They just did not tend to discuss it in terms of the nomenclature they were developing to deal with the nature of conscience. They developed other categories to deal with the nature and scope of prayer and reminded themselves constantly that their distinctions and classifications existed only on a logical level, whereas individual human beings acted as unified, composite wholes. The same cannot be said for the way their teachings were handed down.[26]

5. Another part of the picture has to do with the changing theological horizons of medieval Christianity, which can be described methodologically as a general movement from allegory (as used in monastic theology) to deductive syllogism (as used in scholastic theology) to induction (as used in nominalism and its philosophical progeny). That is to say that the very meaning of theology (i.e., "faith seeking understanding") changed with the developing currents of Western philosophical thought. In patristic and monastic theology, for example, the goal was to become holy through the acquisition of wisdom. Heavily influenced first by a Neoplatonic view of reality (via Augustine of Hippo

---

[26] For Bonaventure's spiritual doctrine, see J. Guy Bougerol, *Introduction to the Works of St. Bonaventure,* trans. José de Vinck (Paterson, N.J.: St. Anthony Guild Press, 1964) 153–62. For Thomas' treatment of prayer and devotion, see *Summa Theologiae* II-II qq. 82–83. For his understanding of the relationship between the gifts of the Spirit and the infused virtues, see Paul J. Wadell, *Friends of God: Virtues and Gifts in Aquinas* (New York: Peter Lang, 1991) 121–36. For the scholastic understanding of the relationship between prayer and theology, see Billy, *Evangelical Kernels* 168. See also B. P. Gaybba, *Aspects of the Medieval History of Theology* (Pretoria: University of South Africa, 1988) 56–57.

[354–430] in the West and Pseudo-Dionysius [c. 500] in the East), this approach emphasized careful contemplative reflection of the sacred texts to discern the hidden meanings placed there by God (e.g., the fourfold senses of Scripture). These symbolic allegories were literary analogues of the Incarnation and corresponded to ideal patterns existing in the mind of God. As such, they pointed the way for the soul's salvific return to its creator that was made possible by the Word made flesh. This approach was symbolic, experiential, practical, and traditional. It highlighted the epistemological role of love and prized the connatural experience of God as the goal of the human sojourn. Augustine of Hippo, the patristic author of late antiquity whose Neoplatonic synthesis of Christian belief had a great impact on the Western medieval outlook, is probably the best representative of this kind of theology. For him, conscience is the voice of God *(vox Dei)* resounding in the heart: "The eternal laws of morality are impressed in the heart of man, 'as the impression of a ring passes into the wax, yet does not leave the ring.'"[27] Prayer, in turn, is a contemplative activity which, through the action of grace, cleanses the mind and frees the will from its bondage to sin and enables it to turn away from mutable goods and attach itself to the one Immutable Good. Viewed in this light, prayer has a vital role to play in the knowledge and performance of the Good and the working out of a person's salvation.

6. Scholastic theology, by way of contrast, arose in the late eleventh and early twelfth centuries and considered the clarification of the content of revelation as its primary goal. Anselm of Canterbury (1033/4–1109) and Peter Abelard (1079–1142) were among the first to use the principles of dialectic to guide their rational investigation into the truths of the faith and are considered the fathers of the scholastic method. Scholastic theology took a major leap forward in the mid-twelfth century with the gradual entry of the Aristotelian corpus into the West by way of Moorish and Arab translators. From that time on and through much of the thirteenth and early fourteenth centuries, attempts were made to integrate the insights of Aristotle with Christian theology. The syllogism of the new Aristotelian logic became one of the major tools of this new endeavor. As described earlier, the scholasticism of the late twelfth and thirteenth centuries was highly creative. Its proponents spanned the spectrum from very conservative, as in Bonaventure, who was more Augustinian in his outlook, to very liberal Latin Averroists, as in Siger of Brabant (1240–1284) and Boethius of

---

[27] Cf. Augustine, *De Trinitate* 14.15.21 (PL 42.1052). The quotation and translation comes from Frederick Copleston, *A History of Philosophy,* vol. 2 (Garden City, N.Y.: Image Books, 1950) 83.

Dacia (dates unknown), who took the views of Aristotle to their extreme logical conclusions (e.g., positing something close to a double truth theory). Albert the Great and Thomas Aquinas held a more middling position, but were viewed by some with suspicion, so much so that in 1277 some of their philosophical and theological positions were on the list of errors condemned by Stephen Tempier, the bishop of Paris.[28] The concern of scholastic theologians with clarifying the "objective" truths of the faith tended to push prayer, considered by them a more "subjective," relational concern, to the periphery of theology (i.e., the act of "faith seeking understanding"). Holiness was no longer considered the primary goal of theological reflection, and prayer was thought of more as an ancillary help rather than an essential element of it. If thinkers such as Bonaventure and Thomas, whose divergent views on conscience were discussed earlier in this chapter, were still able to sustain a creative tension between spirituality and morality (and, in this case, between prayer and conscience), later scholastics would be less successful and, in some cases, downright insistent on their separation.[29]

7. As stated earlier, Scotus' balanced voluntaristic leanings opened the door for the more radical assertions of another Franciscan scholastic theologian. Ockham's nominalist proposals and systematic application of his infamous principal of parsimony knocked a wedge into the cracks of the Neoplatonic synthesis championed by Augustine and the Aristotelian synthesis promulgated by Aquinas—and then proceeded to dismantle them piece by piece. Although these syntheses remained influential forces in the Church throughout the rest of the medieval and modern periods, their larger cultural influence was eclipsed by the Western fascination with particulars. It was from Ockham's criticism of classical Augustinian and Thomistic metaphysics that the worldview of radically singular entities evolved. From this vision, the study of particulars through induction eventually gave rise to the scientific method. On the theological level, Ockham's nominalism rearranged

---

[28] For the condemnations of 1277, see James A. Weisheipl, *Friar Thomas D'Aquino: His Life, Thought, and Work.* With *Corrigenda* and *Addenda* (Washington, D.C.: The Catholic University of America Press, 1983), 333–40. It is worth noting that, throughout their lives, Albert and Thomas were docile to the supervision of the Church hierarchy.

[29] For the main characteristics of scholasticism, see M.-D. Chenu, *Toward Understanding St. Thomas,* trans. M. Landry and D. Hughes (Chicago: Regnery, 1964) 58–69. For a comparison of monastic and scholastic theologies, see Gaybba, *Aspects of the Medieval History of Theology* 52–57. See also Jean Leclercq, *The Love of Learning and the Desire for God,* trans. Catharine Misrahi (3rd ed.; New York: Fordham University Press, 1982) 193–202.

the traditional configuration of the relationship between faith and rea-son. It also placed an extraordinary emphasis on the will, both in God's creation and promulgation of the moral law and in humanity's re-sponse. The inability to prove God's existence or to arrive at the exist-ence of a natural order through rational argumentation widened the gap between theological reflection and devotion and gave rise to a fideistic interpretation of Christian truth and its gradual separation from the conclusions of human reason. Once this occurred, it naturally followed that conscience, now viewed as the rational assessment of one's responsibilities before the law, would have little, if anything, to do with an individual's prayer and devotional life.[30]

8. The nominalism of the late medieval period developed into at least four easily discernible schools and laid the groundwork for later devel-opments in both the religious and secular spheres of Western Europe. The tradition extending from Pierre d'Ailly (1350–1420) to Jean Gerson (c. 1363–1429) and Gabriel Biel (c. 1425–1495) is particularly relevant to our theme. In them, we find a growing stream of theological reflection that culminated in an essentially Pelagian (or, at the very least, semi-Pelagian) emphasis on "doing one's best" *(facere quod in se est)*, while maintaining a deeply devotional mystical theology of the heart. The latter was especially noted for its emphasis on the humble submission of intellect and will to the spiritual authority of Scripture and Church.[31] On the popular level, this growing bifurcation between the rational and the volitional manifested itself in the deep, affective spirituality of the *Devotio moderna* and a growing suspicion of the extended (and often arcane) disputations of late medieval scholasticism. The reactions to these vying tendencies in late medieval spirituality were twofold. On one side, there was the fideistic (i.e., "faith alone") response of the Re-formers, who emphasized humanity's fundamentally corrupted nature

---

[30] For moral obligation in William of Ockham, see Vereecke, *De Guillaume d'Ockham à Saint Alphonse de Liguori*, 149–67. See also Pinckaers, *The Sources of Christian Ethics*, 240–53, esp. 247–49. For an alternative view, see Marilyn McCord Adams, "The Structure of Ockham's Moral Theory," *The Context of Casuistry*, 25–52.

[31] The four schools of late medieval nominalism are: the Ockham-Biel school (in-cluding d'Ailly and Gerson), the English left-wing school of Robert Holcot and Adam Woodham, the right-wing school centered around Gregory of Rimini, and the syncretistic school of Paris. See Heiko Augustinus Oberman, *The Harvest of Medieval Theology: Gabriel Biel and Late Medieval Nominalism* (Durham, N.C.: The Labyrinth Press, 1983) 4. See Oberman also for Biel's doctrine of *facere quod in se est*, his Pelagian tendencies, and the mystical elements in his theology (pp. 132–43, 175–78, 206, 323–60). For arguments attempting to vindicate Biel against the charges of Pelagianism (or semi-Pelagianism), see A. E. McGrath, "The Anti-Pelagian Struc-ture of 'Nominalist' Doctrines of Justification," *Ephemerides Theologiae Lovaniensis* 57 (1981) 107–19.

and the inability of a person to justify himself or herself before God. On the other side, there was the more reserved historical critical focus of Renaissance and Christian humanist thought which, centuries later, would relinquish center stage in the drama of Western culture to the mechanized universe of Enlightened deism. Neither response completely resolved the inherent tensions of the late-medieval worldview. The first looked to revelation and grace to the denigration of the role of reason in human affairs. The second exalted reason first in concert with, but eventually to the virtual exclusion of revelation and grace in the practical circumstances of daily living. Both reactions, moreover, were logical outcomes of late medieval nominalism. Ockham turned to revelation to ascertain the ordained order in the universe. The reformers turned to the Scriptures to discern and then highlight the inherent freedom upon which that order was based (i.e., the law of the Gospel). Ockham, moreover, shunned allegory and syllogism in favor of induction. The proponents of Renaissance and Enlightenment thought used critical reasoning respectively to uncover the treasures of antiquity and to discern a new order of nature that could be verified through observation and formulated into a vast array of rules and laws of nature. As far as prayer and conscience were concerned, the response of the reformers was to pray as though everything depended on God and to work as if everything depended on them. Conscience, as pointed out earlier, focused on inner experience—be it reason's faint judicial light or the inner light of the Holy Spirit—and was looked at primarily through Biblical categories. For the proponents of Renaissance and Enlightenment thought, an exalted understanding of human nature gave central place to the category of conscience, an emphasis arising first from the retrieval of classical sources and later by turning the inductive method inward upon the human subject itself. This latter focus gave rise to the field of philosophical ethics (e.g., as in Kant and Hegel), an area that eventually asserted its own critical autonomy through the radical separation of speculative and practical reason. This modern Western philosophical discipline found little practical use for prayer other than whatever calming effects practices like meditation might have on the mind. These very different ways of relating prayer and conscience continue to influence Western culture down to the present day. Taken together, they represent an ever-widening gap within Western culture between faith and reason, spirituality and morality, prayer and conscience. Only with the dawn of postmodernism have faint signs of a gradual reintegration appeared. Many of the proponents of the reforming spirit have begun to take another look at the insights of late medieval and Counter-Reformation spirituality. Reason's critical eye, in turn, has pried open unforeseen cracks in its own critical assumptions and has recognized the inherent uncertainty of many of its previously thought sacrosanct claims.[32]

9. We have already discussed the general response of the post-Tridentine Church to the positions promulgated first by the Protestant Reformers and later by the proponents of the Enlightenment. Of the five "types" formulated by H. Richard Niebuhr to describe the way Christians have generally understood the relationship between Christ and culture, the Catholic Church's approach to Western culture from the Council of Trent to the second half of the twentieth century was that of "Christ *against* culture" or, as in the case of baroque spirituality, "Christ *above* culture." These attitudes endured for quite some time— and with good reason. When viewed against the backdrop of strong (even hostile) anti-Catholic sentiment in many parts of the world between the late eighteenth and early twentieth centuries (i.e., from the French Revolution to the end of the Second World War), they seem understandable and, in many cases, even appropriate. Only with the post-War era did the currents of hope and active engagement with the world effect a gradual change in the Catholic mindset so that, with the documents of the Second Vatican Council, the understanding of "Christ as the *transformer* of culture" gained a voice and eventually became its guiding paradigm.[33] The Church's understanding of the relationship between prayer and conscience followed along similar lines. Catholic theologians rejected first the reforming doctrine of justification by faith alone, along with its underlying presuppositions about the corrupt human nature and the bondage of the human will, and then the Enlightenment denial of the relevance of prayer in the daily circumstances of life. They went on to adamantly affirm the importance of both conscience *and* prayer in the moral and spiritual lives of the faithful, but did so in a hierarchical and, at least to some eyes, a thoroughly disjunctive way. With the establishment of the seminary system after the Council of Trent, theology was divided into a series of tracts in order to assist teachers both to communicate and to control their classroom material. This eventually led to the development of a number of

---

[32] See James B. Miller, "The Emerging Postmodern World," *Postmodern Theology: Christian Faith in a Pluralist World,* ed. Frederic B. Burnham (New York: Harper Collins, 1989) 1–19. For Catholicism's postmodern opening, see Joe Holland, "The Postmodern Paradigm and Contemporary Catholicism," in David Ray Griffin, William A. Beardslee and Joe Holland, *Varieties of Postmodern Theology,* (Albany, N.Y.: State University of New York Press, 1989) 9–27.

[33] Niebhur's five models are: (1) Christ Against Culture, (2) The Christ of Culture, (3) Christ above Culture, (4) Christ and Culture in Paradox, and (5) Christ the Transformer of Culture. See H. Richard Niebuhr, *Christ and Culture* (New York: Harper & Row, 1951) 45–229.

distinct theological disciplines which theoretically were connected with but which, practically speaking, had very little to do with each other. For our present purposes, it is important to note that practical theology was conveniently divided into a two-tiered hierarchy of moral and spiritual theology: the former dealt with the obligations incumbent upon a person by virtue of the commandments; the latter, with the ascetical and mystical life. The treatment of "conscience" fell quite naturally into the camp of moral theology and that of "prayer" into spiritual theology. As pointed out earlier, in the centuries following Trent, moral theology had developed into a highly sophisticated form of moral casuistry (i.e., case studies). An examination of the writings of some of the prominent moral theologians of this epoch (e.g., Hermann Busenbaum [d. 1668], Daniel Concina [d. 1756], and Alphonsus Liguori [1696–1787]) will find law and conscience at the very center of the discussion. Unfortunately, the nature of moral casuistry and the concentrated focus on the probabilism debate had a restrictive effect on the Church's understanding of the nature and scope of moral theology. All during this time, spiritual theology was concerned with mapping out "the way of perfection." It presupposed the insights of the moral casuistry of the day, but raised its sights by examining what was needed over and above the most basic requirements of the law to achieve perfection. One author describes the resulting dichotomy in the Catholic psyche in this way:

> Much of Catholic *ethics* emphasized love of self, while much of Catholic *spirituality* emphasized denial of self. The former showed how the self benefits in any love for others, while the latter argued that self-forgetfulness and self-denial were necessary for perfection. In the former, concern for self was justified as the way that God created us, while in the latter concern for self was considered a distraction from God-centeredness. In the former, the importance of developing the intellect and freedom was highlighted, while in the latter the quieting of the mind and relinquishing of our own will was encouraged. For ethics, being in relation to the world and therefore having a well-attuned self has been the focus, while for spirituality, especially in the past, the focus has been on forgetting the world and concentrating on God beyond the world.[34]

Even if this contrast between "love of self" and "denial of self" is a little exaggerated, it strikes a sensitive nerve in post-Tridentine outlook and points toward strong tendencies that were very much at work in the

---

[34] Edward Collins Vacek, *Love Human, Love Divine: The Heart of Christian Ethics* (Washington, D.C.: Georgetown, 1994) 200.

relationship between the spiritual and moral spheres of Catholic life. When seen in this light, post-Tridentine moral theology (what the author quoted above refers to as "Catholic ethics") generally emphasized "conscience" as the way of exercising an informed freedom before God, while spiritual theology (referred to above as "Catholic spirituality") looked to the various kinds of prayer (especially *meditatio* and *contemplatio*) as a way of becoming more and more God-centered. That is not to say, of course, that moral theology had nothing to say about prayer or that spiritual theology had nothing to say about conscience. The emphases of these disciplines, however, were clear and somehow converged (with strong countervailing tensions) in the practice and devotional life of the faithful.

10. At the Second Vatican Council, the Church responded to the rapid cultural and technological changes in the world by rethinking the nature and scope of its missionary calling. Rather than reacting against and condemning secular society, the Church sought to dialogue with it, emphasize whatever good it found, and seek to transform it from within. The "inculturation of the Gospel" became the catchword for its new stance toward the various sacred and secular expressions of human culture. This spirit of rapprochement could not be implemented, however, without a corresponding re-examination of the Church's own self-understanding, a process which aimed at rooting theological reflection in the Gospel itself and with a special emphasis on its practical significance for the faithful in their daily lives. The call for the renewal of moral theology along these lines[35] gave official recognition to a process that had already been going on within Catholic moral theology since the end of the Second World War. Another important development in the Council documents was the reaffirmation of conscience as "a man's most secret core, and his sanctuary," that is, "a voice ever calling him to love and to do what is good and to avoid evil."[36] The connection between "conscience" and "love" allowed for a widening of the more legalist concept of conscience as it had been understood in the manualist tradition (a force still present and which had to be reckoned with at the Council). This connection eventually gave rise to the multifaceted approach to conscience discussed earlier, which encouraged Catholic moral theologians to dialogue with currents of secular and religious thought. The use of conscience in the more strictly philosophi-

[35] Catholic Church, Vatican Council II, *Optatam Totius* (Decree on Priestly Formation) 16. See, for example, Austin Flannery, O.P., ed., *Vatican Council II: The Conciliar and Post Conciliar Documents* (Wilmington, Del.: Scholarly Resources, 1975).

[36] Catholic Church, Vatican Council II, *Gaudium et Spes* (Pastoral Constitution on the Church in the Modern World) 16. See, for example, Flannery, ed., *Vatican Council II*.

cal debate on the possibility of an autonomous ethics and in the broader theological attempt to integrate moral theology with the developing discipline of spirituality must be understood in terms of these larger trends within the post-Vatican II Church. One of the important effects of this new approach has been the breakdown of the hierarchical relationship between moral theology and spiritual theology and the gradual understanding of their close, reciprocal relationship. Recent discussions on the close relationship between "conscience," "discernment," "prayer," and "decision-making" verify this claim, as does the recent interest in the spiritual dimension of human reason, and the moral dimensions of prayer.[37] Underscoring the dangers of fideism and an extreme form of rationalism, recent magisterial documents have brought out the importance of seeing a close reciprocal relationship between faith and reason and between Catholic spirituality and moral theology.[38] As such, they set the groundwork for a closer look at the similarly close relationship between conscience and prayer, a topic which later chapters will focus on in depth and imaginatively explore.

Concluding Observations

Our treatment of prayer and conscience in the Christian tradition reveals a complex pattern of relationships. When trying to understand how they have interacted at any particular moment in the Church's history, a great variety of factors must be taken into account: the particular ideas of prayer and conscience in question, the philosophical and theological assumptions supporting them, the particular Christian tradition professing them—to name but a few.

Throughout its history, Eastern Christianity has managed to maintain a closely bound partnership between the prayer and conscience, due mainly to the Neoplatonic outlook that supports its participatory understanding of the relationship between the divine and human, between faith and reason, and between spirituality and morality. Western Christianity, by way of contrast, has experienced a much more complicated

---

[37] See, for example, Gula, *Reason Informed by Faith*, 300–29; Mark O'Keefe, *Becoming Good, Becoming Holy: On the Relationship of Christian Ethics and Spirituality* (Mahwah, N.J.: Paulist Press, 1995) 113–44; Dennis J. Billy, "A 'Spiritual Turn' for Catholic Moral Theology," *Review for Religious* 57 (1998) 595–604; Billy, "Christ's Redemptive Journey and the Moral Dimensions of Prayer," *Studia Moralia* 37 (1999) 127–52; James Keating, "Prayer and Ethics in the Thought of Karl Rahner" *Studies in Spirituality* 7 (1997) 163–77; James Keating, "Prayer and Ethics in the Thought of Hans Urs von Balthasar," *Irish Theological Quarterly* 62 (1996–97) 29–37.

[38] See, for example, John Paul II's *Fides et Ratio*, 36–46.

history, due in large part to the more varied philosophical trends that have gone into shaping it. For the West, the relationship between prayer and conscience has involved a movement from close integration to gradual separation to tentative rapprochement to hopeful reintegration. Prayer, in other words, was at first intimately connected to conscience, then ancillary to it, then merely peripheral to it, then detached from it, then reoriented toward it, and eventually (so it is hoped) reintegrated with it. When seen in this light, the history of the relationship between prayer and conscience in Western Christianity represents just one sub-theme, however important, of a much wider discussion, that is, of the so-called marriage, divorce, and remarriage of Catholic moral theology and spirituality.

When talking about the historical interaction between prayer and conscience in Western Christianity, a number of important qualifying factors must also be taken into account. For one thing, one must be aware that the discussion sometimes borrows images and metaphors from mystical language to describe essentially non-mystical experiences. Calling conscience "the inner voice of God," for example, does not necessarily mean that the reality described is particularly mystical in nature or has anything specifically to do with prayer. It may point merely to the presence of what one author calls a "mystical culture," whereby the language of mysticism has become so deeply ingrained in the sensitivities of a particular culture that it has spilled over comfortably in descriptions of other areas of life.[39] Related to this important caveat is Western theology's hesitation to blur or, worse yet, even confuse the categories of "nature" and "supernature." This caution has enabled theologians to draw out the various dimensions of human existence (in this case, the various levels of moral cognition) and, in doing so, to gain a better insight into what it might mean to be created in the image and likeness of God. A mature discussion of the topic should distinguish between prayer and conscience, yet seek to map out their mutual influence upon each other. This relationship of reciprocity between prayer and conscience can be fully appreciated only when their distinctions are clearly delineated and their various functions examined. Underlying these distinctions is the even more complex question of how human reason itself is conceived of and articulated. This subject will be the focus of the next chapter and will lay the groundwork for a deeper understanding of the reciprocal relationship between prayer and conscience.

---

[39] See Rob Faesen, "What is a Mystical Experience? History and Interpretation," *Louvain Studies* 23 (1998) 243–44.

Chapter Two

Spirit and Reason: Retrieving Lost Connections

"In man there is intellect, consciousness and spirit. There is neither intellect without consciousness nor consciousness without spirit: each subsists in the others and in itself. Intellect expresses itself through consciousness and consciousness is manifested through spirit. In this way man is a dim image of the ineffable and archetypal Trinity, disclosing even now the divine image in which he is created."[1] This passage from *The Philokalia* reveals a very different understanding of the relationship between reason and spirit from what we are used to in the West. Reason, for us, has much to do with "consciousness," but little, if anything, to do with "things spiritual." "Spirit," in turn, has been relegated to the periphery of human experience and plays little if any role in the empirical search for truth. To the extent that we have tried to model it on the empirical sciences, much the same can be said for theology. The danger is especially acute for moral theological reflection, which finds itself today vying in subtle (and often overt) ways with the powerful voices of pragmatist, materialist, and utilitarian thought. The result has been a mounting separation of the spiritual and rational dimensions of the Western psyche, one which ultimately manifests itself in a growing fascination with the irrational and an increased sense of alienation from oneself, others, and God.

---

[1] *The Philokalia: The Complete Text*, trans. G.E.H. Palmer, Philip Sherrard, Kallistos Ware, vol. 4 (Boston: Faber and Faber, 1979) 218.

When seen in this light, the relationship between prayer and conscience is not only a sub-theme of the much wider topic of the connection between spirituality and moral theological reflection, but also of
the underlying link between the constituent elements that make up
such reflection, that is, spirit and reason. In this chapter, we will explore the connection between these two very important dimensions of
human existence. We will argue for a retrieval of reason's ties with the
spiritual, point out its implications for Catholic moral theology, and
show what contributions prayer can make to Catholic moral theological reflection.

Retrieving the Spirit

Given the vast varieties of pseudo-mysticism in the history of Christianity and the great facility with which the name of the Spirit can and
has been invoked as a way of avoiding critical moral reflection, it is
easy to understand how, quite early on, a latent (and, at times, overt)
suspicion grew within orthodox circles of anything that even vaguely
resembled a charismatic rendering of truth by a small "Spirit-filled"
elite. To a large extent, the Church's magisterial structure (i.e., its emphasis on apostolic succession and the role of tradition) took shape as a
result of its struggle against the esoteric (and, at times, laxist) tendencies of Gnostic mysticism, on the one hand, and the rigorist tenets of
Montanist spiritualism, on the other (to name two of the more prominent examples). Historians point to the Church's institutionalization of
the Spirit in the office of the episcopacy and its subsequent control of
the sacramental life of the Christian faithful as the predominant means
by which, down through the centuries, it has safeguarded itself from
similar threats.

One of the unfortunate by-products of this vital process of institutionalization in the life of the Church was the gradual marginalization
of the Spirit from the inner workings of Catholic theological reflection.
As the magisterium became more and more centralized, it consolidated
its hold over what it considered the "authentic" utterings of the Spirit
and helped to create an atmosphere in which theologians, with but few
exceptions, were constrained to pursue their goals within the parameters of increasingly limited notions of rationality. The gradual shift in
Western hermeneutical thought from allegory to syllogism to induction
gives evidence to this effect, as does the roughly parallel movement in
rational theory from analogy to univocity to equivocation. By most
counts, this momentous restructuring of the rational processes of Western thought was as much a function of rising magisterial control of the

sacred as of an ever-changing philosophical terrain (as witnessed in the successive preeminence of Neoplatonic, Aristotelian, and Nominalist thought patterns). Localizing spiritual authority in ecclesiastical institutions, in other words, had the unforeseen effect of gradually disassociating rational discourse from its roots in the intuitive dimension of human existence, that side of human nature most likely to sustain a close experiential rapport with the Spirit.

To speak in broad historical terms, the "despiritualization" of human reason had barely begun in the patristic and monastic traditions of late antiquity and the early middle ages (when the centralization of ecclesiastical power was hardly underway in Rome) and had made recognizable progress during the early scholastic period (near the time of the Gregorian Reform and the Investiture crisis). It was in full swing with the rise of Nominalism in the early fourteenth century (not long after Boniface VIII's proclamation of *Unam sanctam* in 1302) and had reached its highest stage of development during the Age of the Enlightenment (just prior to Vatican I's proclamation of papal infallibility). The inverse historical relationship, moreover, between reason's ever-narrowing scope in Western philosophical thought and the hierarchy's increased centralization of the process of canonization points to a strained and, at times, disjunctive relationship between the spheres of the rational and the sacred in the life of the Church. Putting aside the more difficult task of discerning which historical progression was influenced by which, and recognizing the probability of an ongoing circular relationship between the two (as well as the likely involvement of other discernible historical factors), one cannot help but wonder if the present-day postmodern disillusionment with human reason—itself a reaction against the failed hopes of Reason's coming of age—will herald in an attempt to retrieve reason's lost association with the spiritual. If so, one would also have to wonder if the present tendency in the governing structures of Roman Catholicism toward increased centralization (and, hence, rational control) of "the utterings of the Spirit" is nothing more than a momentary stay in a larger process of decentralization, the forces of which were already at work in the decades preceding the opening of the Second Vatican Council and will probably continue for some time to come.

An Anthropological Turn

Such a retrieval or "reinvestment" of reason's ties with "things spiritual" must proceed from the insights of a sound Christian anthropology. In the present circumstances, the Pauline body/soul/spirit arrangement as formulated in 1 Thess 5:23 proves especially helpful:

"May the God of peace himself sanctify you wholly; and may your spirit and soul and body be kept sound and blameless at the coming of our Lord Jesus Christ." Here, Paul provides an anthropology which construes the human individual as a union of three distinct (albeit intimately related) elements: body *(soma)*, soul *(psyche)*, and spirit *(pneuma)*. "Body" *(soma)*, for Paul, pertains to physical human existence, not in a derogatory sense (as when he opposes spirit *(pneuma)* to flesh *(sarx)*, but as a neutral, yet essential element of the human person. "Soul" *(psyche)*, in turn, indicates the conscious, deliberative dimension of the individual, while "spirit" *(pneuma)*, represents the innermost depths of the individual as it is open to the divine presence and awake to God's Spirit *(Pneuma)*. These elements exist together in the individual and cannot be isolated one from another (as if a human body can be separated from the soul and spirit and still be examined intact). So closely are they related, in fact, that one cannot speak of spirit outside the context of soul and body—and vice versa.[2] Since Paul proposes these anthropological terms while addressing the community of believers in the church at Thessalonica, care must be taken not to isolate his understanding of human existence from either its inherent social context or the life of faith. Account must also be taken of the fact that, given his insistence on their intimate union in the individual, he actually says precious little about how body, soul, and spirit relate to one another in the concrete circumstances of daily living.

Given these significant contextual details (or lack thereof), the following claims appear generally continuous with the main lines of Paul's anthropological vision and offer valuable correctives to our present-day exaggerated emphasis on the rational. (1) In addition to body and soul, an individual can also experience his or her spirit. (2) The mutual relationship between body and soul suggests a similar rapport between soul and spirit. (3) An individual's spirit touches the body through the mediation of the soul. (4) Generally speaking, the Holy Spirit touches an individual by communicating its grace first to a person's spirit and then through the spirit to a person's soul and body. (5) God and the individual can enjoy a close interpersonal rapport by virtue of their communing spirits. (6) Individuals relate to one another on the level of body, soul, *and* spirit. (7) The Spirit unites the Body of Christ, the Church, not only theologically (i.e., to God), but also anthropologically (i.e., to one another). (8) Because of the hierarchical spirit-soul-body relationship that makes an individual a single integrated

---

[2] For this reason they differ vastly from the trichotomized anthropology of Platonic philosophy. See A. M. Festuguère, "La trichotomie de 1 Th 5:23 et la philosophie grecque," *Recherches de science religieuse* 20 (1930) 385–415.

whole, it does so first on the level of human spirit and then out (by way of *redundantia*) to the other dimensions of human existence.

Elicited from the Pauline anthropology of 1 Thess 5:23, these anthropological claims provide the basic parameters by which a discussion about reason's "spiritual renewal" may proceed. Key to this discussion is the need for all theologians (and for moral theologians in particular) to recognize the competence (and the limits) of reason's rule. Just as reason extends to the body through its ordering of the passions (and is thereby "enfleshed"), so does the spirit extend to the soul (the seat of the rational faculty) by means of its quiet intuiting presence. Clearly, both movements have moral significance that must be taken into account for the future of moral theology.

The Criteria of Reason's Spiritual Rebirth

How might such a relationship be construed? Without exhausting the possibilities, the following list seeks to provide some basic guidelines for discerning the genuine ways in which reason and spirit mutually influence one another.

1. An anthropological relationship of circularity exists between spirit and reason, that is, the insights of one complement the scope and competence of the other in such a way that, when taken together, their interaction generates a field of understanding unique to themselves and which neither would be fully capable of penetrating on its own. Spirit brings intuition and moments of keen insight to the movement of discursive thought; reason articulates through language something of the inexpressible utterings of the human spirit. Authentic theological reflection taps into this relationship of circularity and allows it to open up for each succeeding generation the meaning of the symbols of the Christian faith.

2. The spirit influences the mind through prayer—and vice versa. When a person's spirit communes with God's Spirit, there is a natural reverberation (however so slight) onto the other anthropological dimensions of human existence. This subtle influence, which will become a veritable overflowing *(redundantia)* in the beatific vision, strengthens the transcendent orientation of an individual's rational operation. A "spiritual" person tends to concentrate on holy things and seeks to view all things with the mind of Christ. In this respect, prayer (and contemplative prayer in particular) plays a transforming rather than merely ancillary role in reason's spiritual homecoming.

3. The human spirit is not "irrational," but "suprarational." It does not ask reason to go against its own internal principles, but seeks continually to broaden reason's scope by providing intuited insights that

challenge previously unquestioned (and possibly fallacious) arguments. When reason is in tune with wholesome human spirit (and even more so when it is in touch with God's Spirit), it is constantly prompted to reach beyond itself and to stretch the boundaries with which it normally functions. This extended range is a welcomed corrective to that narrowing univocity which nowadays so often masquerades as the sole legitimate face of rational inquiry.

4. Theologians who reintegrate spirit and reason demonstrate a guarded yet profound respect for Church authority. The gradual marginalization of spirit from the center of theological reflection that came, at least in part, as a result of magisterial centralization and control of the sacred, does not mean that a "respiritualized" reason will ignore or (worse yet) outwardly disdain the valuable hermeneutical role the magisterium has played in the history of the Catholic Tradition. On the contrary, a reintegration of spirit and reason should bring about an even closer working relationship between theologians (in their concern for reasoned clarity and the exploration of the faith) and the magisterium (in its concern for the preservation and purity of the faith). While both may not always agree, a close working relationship between them will provide helpful correctives against the extremes of over-rationalization and pseudo-mysticism that can all too often get in the way (and even obscure) sound theological reflection.

5. A closer working rapport between a person's spirit and reason will require a reintegrated understanding of the various theological disciplines, especially between dogmatic, moral, and spiritual theology. The unfortunate breakup of theology in recent centuries into separate and highly specialized disciplines can itself be understood as a symptom of reason's ongoing despiritualization over time. A renewed or "respiritualized" understanding of reason will operate successfully only in a context that seeks to preserve the unity of theology in the midst of its highly specialized and, at times, seemingly disconnected parts.

6. Renewing reason's link with the spirit will also move a person's sense of vocation to the center of theological reflection. No longer will theology be construed as something existing "in the abstract," as if proceeding outside the theologian's own personal and communal faith experience. Any presentation and consequent systematization of the symbols of the faith will be valid only to the extent that it remains faithful to and authentically expresses the deepest sense of a person's call in life before God through the Church, and in the world. One's reflection on God, in other words, must take place in the context of one's sense of self in the presence of God and the community of believers.

7. The reason/spirit relationship sheds greater light on the importance of there being a continuity between the theologian's professional

work and his or her moral behavior. Sound theological reflection stems from a stable interplay between spirit and reason. It reflects the contours of a person's call from God in this life and reaches its fullest expression when it is enfleshed in the concrete circumstances of a person's daily existence. This cannot happen, however, if reason is deprived of all access to the nourishing roots of the spirit, where the human person communes with the Spirit of God through a grace that is freely given and freely received. Sound theological reflection challenges the theologian to integrate reason and spirit, theological discourse and personal sanctity. The Church needs theologians who want to be saints, who admit this desire without false humility, and who bring this desire to the forefront of their theological inquiry.

8. Finally, a reintegration of spirit and reason would sustain a healthy tension within theological reflection between "theology as science" (i.e., the methodological rational investigation, formulation, and systematization of Christian belief) and "theology as art" (i.e., the esthetic use of image, narrative, and symbol to convey an intuitive grasp of the divine mystery). Reason's desire to verify complements the spirit's yearning for mystery—and vice versa. Together, they provide useful correctives to the tendencies of over-rationalization and exaggerated rhetoric, which lessen theology's scope by seeking to turn it into something it is not and should not be. Theology is more than science and more than art. It is science *and* art, a rare "field-encompassing"[3] discipline which touches all areas of human knowledge in its attempt to convey the meaning of the Christian faith to each successive generation. By nurturing this tension, theological reflection equips itself with a way of expressing the faith ever anew yet ever faithful to the Church's theological tradition. New and creative insights emerge from the tradition precisely in this way, thereby allowing it to expand its theological horizons and to move forward.

Implications for Moral Theology

The above criteria represent just some of the ways in which a deeper understanding of the relationship between spirit and reason would change the way in which theology itself is conceived and carried out.

---

[3] The notion of a "field-encompassing" discipline comes from Van A. Harvey, *The Historian and the Believer: The Morality of Historical Knowledge and Christian Belief* (Philadelphia: The Westminister Press, 1966) 81–82. A similar application to spirituality appears in Sandra M. Schneiders, "Spirituality in the Academy," *Theological Studies* 50 (1989) 692.

As one might expect, they have very concrete implications for the future of moral theology.

1. Moral theology would be challenged to break out of its hylomorphic rendering of the human (i.e., moral) act that has set the parameters for serious discussion within the Catholic tradition since the time of Aquinas. A human action is more than just an expression of body (as the object of the external action) and mind (as the intentional movement of deliberated will). Greater sensitivity must be given in future moral theological reflection to the influence which a person's *spirit* brings to moral action. A good place to begin would be to apply the insights of Aquinas' teaching on grace (which, interestingly enough, he considers under "The New Law" at the end of his treatment of the fundamental principles of morality, that is, *Summa Theologiae* I-II q.109-114) to the Pauline rendering of human anthropology as body *(soma)*, soul *(psyche)*, and spirit *(pneuma)*. In such an application, the continuity upheld by Aquinas between being and action as a result of the body/ soul anthropology he adopts from Aristotle would necessitate a three dimensional change in focus corresponding to the height and width and depth of Pauline anthropology.

2. For this to occur, a shift must take place in the understanding of the nature and role of rationality in current moral theological reflection. In its attempt in recent years to model itself after the empirical and social sciences, theology in general (and moral theology in particular) has adopted an univocal understanding of rational inquiry that prevents a balanced interplay of reason and spirit from entering into the legitimate bounds of serious theological reflection. The result has been an unfortunate narrowing (some would say "impoverishment") of theology's rightful scope. The current deadlock in the deontologist/proportionalist discussion is but one symptom of this reductive theological undertaking. Locked in heated debate over the nature of the rational parameters of moral decision-making, both sides have turned moral theology away from the ongoing and dedicated search for practical wisdom (otherwise known as "prudence") and focused instead on a highly rarified form of academic (some would say "armchair") problem-solving. The growing interest in virtue ethics and in the relationship between spirituality and morality indicates that this badly needed shift is already taking place.

3. Since the spirit expresses itself more through images than in the "clear and distinct" ideas of rational discourse, future moral theological discussion will have to develop a greater sensitivity to the ethical content of humanity's symbolic expressions. To modify Aristotle's definition: Man is not just a *rational* but also a *symbolic* animal. In developing this sensitivity, moral theology will draw closer to the arts than

ever before (at least within recent memory) and begin to effect a transformation of the genres and literary style in which it expresses itself. It will also spark a renewed interest in the ethical content of the images and symbols found in the Scriptures and the Church's liturgy.

4. Future moral theological discussion will develop close ties with the three levels of Christian spirituality: (1) the experiential, (2) the sapiential, and (3) the analytical.[4] Ethical knowledge will be understood as something to be garnered from the whole of human experience (i.e., throughout the body/soul/spirit continuum) with special emphasis given to the social aspects of human moral-spiritual discourse and to the role of prayer and discernment in moral decision-making. This heightened awareness of the spiritual aspects of its theological heritage will give moral theology a deeper awareness of its own most distinctive traits and enable it to make serious contributions in discussions with other ethical traditions (e.g., dialogue with the Hindu, Moslem, and Buddhist viewpoints).

5. Given its decision to approach moral knowledge through a reintegrated understanding of the rapport between spirit and reason, Catholic moral theology would do best to enter into future dialogue with other ethical traditions—be they philosophical and/or theological—not by seeking a least common methodological denominator (usually fully acceptable to neither side), but by maintaining without compromise its position on the close anthropological (and hence ethical) connection between human reason and human spirit. It is precisely on this level that an answer to the question of the existence of an autonomous Christian ethics will be found.

Implications for Prayer

The above reflections on the relationship between spirit and reason help bring to the fore the specific moral dimensions of prayer. For Christians, morality can be detached from the spiritual life only in the abstract. In real life, it must be intimately connected to a living faith in Jesus Christ.[5] Prayer itself is a human action made possible by the

[4] These levels of spirituality are developed under a slightly different nomenclature in Walter H. Principe, "Toward Defining Spirituality," *Studies in Religion/ Sciences religieuses* 12 (1983) 135–36. See also Walter H. Principe, "Spirituality, Christian," *The New Dictionary of Catholic Spirituality,* ed. Michael Downey (Collegeville, Minn.: The Liturgical Press, 1993) 931–38.

[5] "The criterion of what is Christian, the distinctive Christian feature—this holds both for dogmatics and consequently also for ethics—is not an abstract something nor a Christ idea, not a Christology nor a Christocentric system of ideas: it is *this*

movement of God's grace in our lives. It embraces every dimension of our anthropological makeup—the physical, the emotional, the mental, the spiritual, and the social—and, as such, serves three important functions: the teleological, the instrumental, and the anthropological.

1. *The Teleological.* Prayer helps us to focus on God as our final end. It does so by bringing this fundamental relationship of our lives to the forefront and by helping us to orient everything we do in life toward it. The more we pray, the more God becomes the focus of all we do. The Apostle's injunction "to pray without ceasing" (1 Thess 5:17) reminds us of our need to allow God to be the firmly focused goal of our daily activity. Our final end, in other words, has important ramifications for how we live our lives. Prayer is the great means of salvation precisely because it helps us to focus more firmly on God as our final end. The gifts of the Spirit and the life of the infused virtues cannot be viewed outside of this underlying teleological framework. To do so, would be to totally misconstrue the ends and means of the Christian moral life.[6]

2. *The Instrumental.* If we ever wish to reach our final end, we can do so only through appropriate rational means, that is, by living a virtuous life. We become virtuous, however, not through *our* efforts alone, but by cooperating with God's grace in a long, arduous process of conversion. Prayer is essential to this process. It keeps us in a living, dynamic relation with the ground of our being, which gradually effects a conversion in us on every level of our anthropological makeup. Without prayer, we have no hope of truly discerning what to do in a given situation, let alone implementing it in an appropriate way. With prayer, we are able to both discern and implement the appropriate means for succeeding in our spiritual journey.[7]

3. *The Anthropological.* Prayer must involve every aspect of our lives in its teleological and instrumental functions. It does so by integrating for us the various dimensions of human existence so that the "dissonance" we experience deep within ourselves might be healed and one

---

concrete *Jesus as the Christ, as the standard.*" See Hans Küng, "The Criterion for Deciding What Is Christian," *Introduction to Christian Ethics: A Reader,* eds. Ronald P. Hamel and Kenneth R. Himes (New York/New Jersey: Paulist Press, 1989) 127.

[6] For the dynamics of the infused virtues, see Romanus Cessario, *The Moral Virtues and Theological Ethics* (Notre Dame/London: University of Notre Dame Press, 1991) 117–25.

[7] See, for example, the connections established among the beatitudes, the gifts of the Spirit and the petitions of the Our Father in Augustine, *De Sermone Domini in Monte secundum Matthaeum* 2.11.38 (PL 34:1286). For commentary, see Servais Pinckaers, *The Sources of Christian Ethics,* trans. Mary Thomas Noble (3rd ed.; Edinburgh: T. & T. Clark, 1995) 155–58. For how prayer draws us to our final end in God, see Pseudo-Dionysius, *On the Divine Names* 3.1 (PG 3:679-80). On the efficacy of prayer, see Thomas Aquinas, *Summa contra Gentiles* 3.95-96.

day elevated by the power of Christ's Spirit. We need to pray to God, therefore, with our bodies (e.g., through gesture and song), with our emotions (e.g., by identifying and then by expressing to God exactly how we feel), with our minds (e.g., through spiritual reading and by meditating on the mysteries of the faith), with our spirits (e.g., by resting in silence before an icon or a burning candle), and with others (e.g., through shared prayer and prayer meetings). All of these dimensions of prayer come together in the Liturgy which, when celebrated properly, gives us an opportunity to offer up to God every aspect of our anthropological makeup.[8]

Since all of us are unique individuals, it should not be surprising for us to learn that each of us tends to favor one or more of the dimensions of our anthropological makeup (and hence type of prayer) over others. For this reason, it is important that each of us find the right rhythm that, at one and the same time, incorporates both our own personal inclinations to prayer and all the other anthropological dimensions of human existence. We must strive, in other words, to find the right balance of prayer in our lives that will address every level of our being, while at the same time remaining true to our deepest selves.[9]

As we do this, it is normally a good idea for us to take a look at those aspects of our anthropological makeup (and, by analogy, those forms of prayer) that we tend to overlook and perhaps even purposely ignore. The more we neglect to express a side of us to God in prayer, the more difficult will it be for the Spirit to heal it and make it resonate with the other aspects of our being.[10] The result would be a typically "qualified" expression of prayer, where we hold something back from God because we do not wish to face up to some aspect of our lives or from fear of what might be asked from us. Such "qualified prayer" has a detrimental effect on the teleological and instrumental functions of prayer, since it tends to blur our focus on God as our final end and withhold a part of our anthropological makeup from the purview of virtuous activity.

[8] For the relationship between prayer and the anthropological dimensions of human existence, see Dennis J. Billy, *Evangelical Kernels: A Theological Spirituality of the Religious Life* (Staten Island, N.Y.: Alba House, 1993) 167–84. For the relationship between theology and worship, see Avery Dulles, *The Craft of Theology: From Symbol to System* (New York: Crossroad, 1995) 197–210. For the moral and spiritual dimensions of the Liturgy, see below n. 22.

[9] See Billy, *Evangelical Kernels,* 174.

[10] This insight expresses the classical Thomistic doctrine of *redundantia:* "The union with God glorifies the soul; the glorified soul expresses itself in a glorified body; the glorified body is endowed with a glorified creation." See Carlo Leget, *Living with God: Thomas Aquinas on the Relation Between Life on Earth and "Life" After Death* (Leuven: Peeters, 1997) 211. See also Aquinas, *Summa Theologiae* I-II q.4 a.6 resp.

Prayer and Catholic Moral Theological Reflection

The teleological, instrumental, and anthropological dimensions of prayer have obvious repercussions for a proper understanding of the nature of Catholic moral theological reflection. Three, in particular, stand out.

1. *The Right Questions.* All Catholic moral theological reflection, even that dealing with the most sophisticated contemporary ethical issues needs, sooner or later, to address three basic questions: (1) Does it help us to focus on our final end, that is, God? (2) Does it help to constitute virtuous behavior? And (3) Does it contribute to the further integration of the various anthropological dimensions of human existence? In and of itself, prayer may not be able to answer any of these questions for the Catholic moral theologian as he or she struggles with some of the very difficult ethical issues confronting today's Catholic faithful. One of the things it can do, however, is to guarantee that these important questions are raised and kept in mind (at least peripherally) as the act of theological reflection takes place. In this respect, it provides an important spiritual moral backdrop against which the act of Catholic moral theological reflection occurs.[11]

2. *Responding to a Call.* The vocational dimensions of Catholic moral theological reflection must also be taken into account. Such reflection is done by individuals and groups entrusted with a specific task within the Church. That task has enormous responsibilities attached to it, for it requires not only that they "think with the Church," but also *for the very good of the Church* be willing to look at "the Church's thinking" with a critical eye. As Christians, Catholic moral theologians are called to submit their entire lives to God through the activity of prayer. As moral theologians, they need to orient the activity of theological reflection to the same end. Their very sanctity depends on it. Their moral theological reflection is not something they do "in addition to" their lives as ordinary Christians, but flows from it as one of the major means through which they will work out their salvation. For this very reason, prayer has an intimate connection with what they do. Because they fulfill a very specific task within the Church as teachers and researchers of Catholic moral truth, they need to pray for guidance and discernment as they struggle to find concrete solutions to the complex moral problems of the day. To do so adequately, they must be firmly rooted in the Catholic theological tradition, in creative dialogue with the pressing

---

[11] For the relationship between prayer and the Christian's moral sense, see Enda McDonagh, *Gift and Call: Towards a Christian Theology of Morality* (Dublin: Gill and Macmillan, 1975) 90–92.

problems and challenges of the world, and people imbued with a deep spirit of prayer.[12]

3. *A Broader View.* Finally, the various dimensions of prayer underscore the interrelated nature of the human person, and challenges Catholic moral theologians to widen their understanding of what constitutes the rational basis of moral theological reflection. From this perspective, the connatural knowledge of contemplative prayer, the theoretical and practical insights gained from spiritual reading, the emotional experience received from a prayerful use of the imagination, the "body knowledge" coming from such practices as fasting and abstinence, and the "sense of the faith" imbibed by immersing oneself in the liturgical traditions of the Church, all have something to contribute to the "rational" process known as "moral theological reflection." Theological reflection is fundamentally an incarnational activity rooted in the person and in the traditions of the religious community of which he or she forms a part. The integrating function of prayer can help theologians in general (and Catholic moralists in particular) to expand their understanding of what constitutes rational reflection in the act of "faith seeking understanding" *(fides quaerens intellectum).* It does so, first and foremost, by performing its important integrating work of turning anthropological "dissonance" into anthropological "resonance," a process that cannot be understood apart from the underlying context of ongoing individual and communal conversion. It also does so by pointing to the great variety of "prayer rhythms" that help preserve the uniqueness of the individual in the face of the common anthropological features shared with the rest of humanity, an insight which goes very well with the well-established notion that there is not one but a variety of models of moral theological reflection within the Catholic tradition.[13]

The Moral Dimensions of Prayer

The above observations on human action and the nature of Catholic moral theological reflection enable us now to outline some of the underlying moral values that a life of prayer will reinforce in a person's life. The list, while by no means exhaustive, provides us with a sense of some of the ways in which prayer can help us to be aware of the ethical dimensions of Christian living.

[12] For a discussion of vocation in the life of the theologian, see Lynda Robitaille, "A Sense of Vocation," *Spirituality and Morality,* ed. Dennis Billy and Donna Orsuto (Mahwah, N.J.: Paulist, 1996) 49–66.

[13] This variety could be easily adapted from the general models of theological reflection found in Raymond F. Collins, *Models of Theological Reflection* (Lanham, Md.:

1. *The Relational Backdrop of Christian Moral Decision-Making*. To begin with, the dialogical nature of prayer brings to the fore the relational foundations of all of Christian life. A deepened relationship with God in prayer calls a person to raise the quality of his or her relationship with others. As a person becomes more and more intimate with God, he or she begins to realize that what is really important in life ultimately has to do with relationships: within oneself, with other individuals, within community, among nations, with the environment, etc. Having a close relationship with the relational God invites a person to examine the status and meaning of all the other relationships that touch his or her life. In this respect, the vertical dimension (i.e., human/ divine) of Christian prayer is intrinsically connected to a horizontal one (i.e., human/human and human/non-human). Love of God is intrinsically related to love of neighbor (and one might also add, love of the earth). Prayer helps a person to recognize the importance of his or her relationships and of taking them into account in the concrete decisions of daily life.[14]

2. *The Transformative Nature of Christian Moral Decision-Making*. Prayer also brings to the fore the relationship between conversion and virtuous living. Authentic prayer brings about a gradual change in people's lives. This process of change begins in the innermost sanctums of the human heart and eventually flows out into the other anthropological dimensions of a person's life. The slow movement from anthropological "dissonance" to "resonance" manifests itself in a person's deeds and inner attitudes. These, in turn, further deepen the experience of conversion and encourage a person to an even deeper life of prayer. Prayer, in other words, effects conversion which, in turn, brings about a change in a person's interior dispositions and outward actions. A deeply rooted habit of prayer not only deepens a person's relationship with God, but also helps to effect an interior change of heart that

---

University of America Press, 1984). For the variety of definitions of Christian ethics, see Pinckaers, *The Sources of Christian Ethics*, 4–13. For a philosophical discussion of the rationality of traditions, see Alasdair MacIntyre, *Whose Justice? Which Rationality?* (Notre Dame: University of Notre Dame Press, 1988) 349–69. For a discussion of tradition in the context of moral theology, see Brian V. Johnstone, "Faith and Reason in Morals: A Polyphony of Traditions," *Studia Moralia* 35 (1997) 261–82.

[14] "As a man is, so he prays. We make ourselves what we are by the way we address God." See Thomas Merton, *No Man Is an Island* (Garden City, N.Y.: Image, 1955) 46. For the importance of relationships in moral theology and spirituality, see also Kevin O'Neil, "Forming Right Relationships," in *Spirituality and Morality*, 97–111; Mark O'Keefe, *Becoming Good, Becoming Holy: On the Relationship of Christian Ethics and Spirituality* (Mahwah, N.J.: Paulist Press, 1995) 75–90.

gradually brings a person's thoughts, words, and actions in conformity with Gospel values.[15]

3. *The Narrative Basis of Christian Morality.* A Christian's moral decisions should flow from his or her living relationship with God, which can only be nourished by a dedicated life of prayer. The ensemble of a person's prayer experiences constitutes an important memory that has a great impact on his or her outlook on life and process of moral decision-making. When taken together, these experiences form the narrative backdrop against which he or she understands the nature of what it means to live "in the Spirit." The more a person brings to God the concrete problems and concerns of his or her life, the more will the process of spiritual and moral discernment be rooted in a sense of the presence of God's providential care. In doing so, an individual begins to view his or her moral life as intimately involved with the story of his or her ongoing relationship with God. That story cannot be fully understood, however, apart from the larger narrative of the person's relationship to God's People, the Church, and its ongoing salvific mission in the world. These interweaving histories—of a person's relationship with God and with God's People—provide the Christian with the narrative context within which he or she conceives of, approaches, and seeks to resolve the moral dilemmas of his or her life.[16]

4. *The Relevance of Scripture for the Christian Moral Life.* The centrality of Scripture for Christian prayer has an effect on a person's moral outlook. Scripture provides not only explicit content for the Christian moral vision (the Decalogue [Deut 5:1-22], the Golden Rule [Matt 22:37-39], the Beatitudes [Matt 5:1-12]), but also a narrative point of departure for developing a contemplative outlook on life. Well-established prayer forms such as the *lectio divina* encourage the person at prayer to break open the Word of God and to listen to it with the heart. Through such practices, the Scriptures mediate an experience of the Spirit in one's life and invite a person to allow that Word to grow within him or her and become flesh. A person who listens to the Word of God in the Scriptures in a contemplative manner gradually carries that outlook to the rest of his or her affairs. Since contemplation is an

---

[15] See O'Keefe, *Becoming Good, Becoming Holy*, 27–43, 113–24; Brian V. Johnstone, "The Dynamics of Conversion," *Spirituality and Morality*, 32–48.

[16] "So in allowing ourselves to adopt and be adopted by a particular story, we are in fact assuming a set of practices which will shape the ways we relate to our world and destiny." See Stanley Hauerwas, Richard Bondi, and David Burrell, *Truthfulness and Tragedy: Further Investigations in Christian Ethics* (Notre Dame: University of Notre Dame Press, 1977) 36. For the social dimensions of narrative and Christian ethics, see Stanley Hauerwas, *A Community of Character: Toward a Constructive Christian Social Ethic* (Notre Dame, Ind.: University of Notre Dame Press, 1981) 9–35.

essential feature of happiness (even in our present imperfect state), it follows that it will have much to offer a person as he or she strives to make sense of his or her role in a quickly changing world.[17]

5. *The Epistemological Role of Love in the Christian Moral Life*. A life of prayer also gives the Christian a deeper appreciation of the epistemological role of love in his or her moral outlook. Through prayer, a person not only professes belief in a personal God, but also comes to an intimate knowledge of him. This knowledge is connatural rather than conceptual and entails not a factual knowledge of the faith, but a loving penetration into the divine mystery that sustains it. As a person persists in prayer, he or she draws closer to God in charity, that is, through an intimate union of the divine and human wills (on the level of soul) and the divine and human spirits (on the even deeper level of *pneuma*). This union has been likened to "a certain kind of friendship" and bears the threefold marks of benevolence, reciprocity, and mutual indwelling. As friendship with God, charity informs the other virtues and conveys an intuitive appreciation of the faith. This appreciation manifests itself, first and foremost, in a deeper desire for conversion of life and a willingness to adhere more firmly to the *lex nova* of Christ's abiding Spirit.[18]

6. *A Broader Understanding of Conscience*. The new relationship effected between the Holy Spirit and the human spirit by Christ's redemptive journey allows for a broader notion of moral conscience. Rather than the classical two-tiered understanding of conscience as a judgment of the practical intellect (i.e., conscience) supported by an intuitive understanding of the fundamental principles of the moral law within the very structures of human moral cognition (i.e., *synderesis*), a third tier can be added by which the Spirit touches our own spirits (i.e., through grace) and confides in us through its internal promptings a deeper insight into the moral requirements of the *lex nova*. At this level, the classical distinctions between the natural (i.e., creaturely, [to be]redeemed, [to be]sanctified) and supernatural (i.e., Creative, Redeeming,

---

[17] For the priority of contemplation even in the state of imperfect happiness, see Thomas Aquinas, *Summa Theologiae* I-II q.3 a.5 resp. For fostering a contemplative attitude toward life, see William A. Barry and William J. Connolly, *The Practice of Spiritual Direction* (Minneapolis, Minn.: The Seabury Press, 1982) 46–64.

[18] See Aquinas, II-II q. 23, a.1., resp.; a.8, resp.; q. 24 a.2 resp. For a discussion of the epistemological role of love, see B. P. Gaybba, *Aspects of the Medieval History of Theology: Twelfth to Fourteenth Centuries* (Pretoria: University of South Africa, 1988) 32–43. For a discussion of knowledge through connaturality, see William Johnston, *Mystical Theology: The Science of Love* (London: Harper Collins, 1995) 50–59. For a discussion of charity as friendship with God, see Paul J. Wadell, *Friendship and the Moral Life* (Notre Dame, Ind.: University of Notre Dame Press, 1989) 120–41; Paul J. Wadell, *The Primacy of Love: An Introduction to the Ethics of Thomas Aquinas* (Mahwah, N.J.: Paulist, 1992) 63–78.

Sanctifying) orders are maintained, but in a way that is sensitive to the eschatological (already-but-not-yet) orientation of the new creation effected by Christ's redemptive action. When seen in this light, the first glimmerings of the new creation are found in the fundamental anthropological reorientation which Christ's mediating divine-human prayer from the cross effects in the deepest levels of human existence. Because of that prayer, the Holy Spirit now yearns for transcendence within the human heart, goading and prompting it to a deeper and more certain knowledge of the most basic of Gospel values (See chapter four for more details).[19]

7. *The Relevance of Spirituality for the Christian Moral Life.* A life of prayer also enables a person to appreciate the close connections that exist between Christian spirituality and morality. Such connections come through especially when spirituality is understood as a "field-encompassing" discipline embracing "those aspects of a person's living faith or commitment that concern his or her striving to attain the highest ideal or goal."[20] When seen in this light, both spirituality and morality have the same ultimate end (i.e., God) and prayer is a significant means used by each of them for achieving that end. What is more, each can be understood as operating on three distinct (yet related) levels of legitimate inquiry: personal experience, teachings, and academic study. These parallels point not only to the complementary nature of Christian spirituality and morality, but also to their common unifying ground. Prayer shares in this unified complementarity not so much by providing explicit content for either of these fields to work on (regardless of the level being referred to), but by informing the process of "faith seeking understanding" itself in an ancillary or even intrinsic manner.[21]

---

[19] For the two levels of conscience, see Joseph Ratzinger, *Conscience and Truth* (Dallas, Tex.: Knights of Columbus, 1991) 23–32. For the relationship between conscience and the Holy Spirit, see Servais Pinckaers, "L'instinct et l'Esprit au coeur de l'éthique chrétienne," in *Novitas et veritas vitae: aux sources du renouveau de la morale chrétienne*, ed. Carlos-Josaphat Pinto de Oliveira (Paris: Editions du Cerf, 1991) 213–23. For Christ's redemptive journey and the new relationship effected between the Holy Spirit and the human spirit, see Dennis J. Billy, "Christ's Redemptive Journey and the Moral Dimensions of Prayer," *Studia Moralia* 37 (1999) 127–37. This "spiritual" dimension of conscience, moreover, would effect every level of the contemporary understanding of conscience as a capacity, a process, and a judgment (cf. chap. one).

[20] See Sandra M. Schneiders, "Spirituality in the Academy," *Theological Studies* 50 (1989) 692; Principe, "Spirituality, Christian," *Dictionary of Catholic Spirituality*, 139.

[21] See Billy, *Evangelical Kernels*, 167-70; Principe, "Spirituality, Christian," *Dictionary of Catholic Spirituality*, 135–37; John Macquarrie, "Prayer and Theological Reflection," *The Study of Spirituality*, eds. C. Jones, G. Wainwright et al. (Oxford and New York: Oxford University Press, 1986) 584–87.

8. *The Relevance of Liturgy for the Christian Moral Life. Lex orandi, lex credendi, lex vivendi.* Christian prayer finds its fullest expression in the Liturgy, the prayer of the Church universal. There, the Church is most at home and most deeply expresses itself to God the Father, through the action of Christ, and in the Spirit. The Liturgy, and the Eucharist in particular, lies at the very heart of the Church. There, every anthropological dimension of human existence is addressed and brought under the recreative action of God's redemptive grace. There, all the major forms of prayer—adoration, praise, thanksgiving, petition, intercession—find expression and are addressed to God and offered up on the basis of humanity's eschatological participation in the new creation. When at prayer, the Church gathers all of humanity into itself under the headship of Christ and receives not only his intercession on the world's behalf before the Father, but also the help of his Spirit in seeking to resolve the concrete problems facing the world today. This action of the Spirit in the world is not reserved for abstract questions of an ethereal spiritual nature, but engages humanity in the most complex and perplexing dilemmas that it faces. It does so by reminding us that love, not hatred, forms the very basis of all reality and should also be at the basis of all human relationships.[22]

9. *An Appreciation of Prayer as a Basis for Ecumenical and Interreligious Ethics.* Christ's redemptive journey restored harmony to humanity's anthropological makeup and reestablished the bond between the human spirit and the Spirit of God. His anguished prayer from the cross resonates now within every human heart and manifests itself in the yearning of God's Spirit within our own. When seen in this light, his deep, heartfelt yearning for transcendence is the common ground that binds all of humanity together in its common spiritual quest. It forms an important point of departure for all aspects of ecumenical and interreligious dialogue and opens up new horizons for further collaboration on the development of a common religious ethic uniting all of the world's great religions. All of this has become possible because, in Christ, theology and anthropology have now become intimately related. God's fullest revelation to humanity is now manifest deep within

---

[22] For the moral and spiritual dimensions of Christian worship, see O'Keefe, *Becoming Good, Becoming Holy,* 91–109; Jan Michael Joncas, "The Church at Prayer," *Dictionary of Catholic Spirituality* 80–96; Enda McDonagh, *Invitation and Response: Essays in Christian Moral Theology* (Dublin: Gill and Macmillan, 1972) 96–108; Donald E. Saliers, "Liturgy and Ethics: Some New Beginnings," *Journal of Religious Ethics* 7 (1979) 173–89; Sergio Bastianel, Prayer in Christian Moral Life, trans. Bernard Hoose (Middlegreen, Slough, England: St. Paul Publications, 1988), 69–87; Geoffrey Wainwright, *Doxology: A Systematic Theology* (London: Epworth Press, 1980) 399–434. See also Dulles, *The Craft of Theology,* 197–210.

the human heart. God's heartfelt cry from the cross now resonates within every human heart where the Spirit cries out "with groanings that cannot be expressed in speech (Rom 8:26)."[23]

10. *An Appreciation for the Healing and Elevating Role of the Spirit.* Finally, prayer reminds us that the healing and elevation of humanity (on whatever anthropological level) ultimately comes about through the action of the Spirit in our lives. This insight is an important corrective for the traditional "commandment-oriented" presentation of the moral life. Placing prayer at the center of Christ's redemptive journey helps us to see the moral life as an aspect of the one journey in which all of us are called to participate. It reminds us that the Christian moral life loses its character and inner dynamism once it is taken out of the context of the ongoing call to conversion. What is more, it helps us to recognize our own inability to do what the Lord asks of us in our lives and hence our need to ask for his help. Prayer helps us to get in touch with our inner weakness and to humbly ask God for a change of heart. It bids us to turn to God at all times and to ask for the grace to respond to promptings of the Spirit in our lives and to use its gifts for the good of others. Through prayer, the Spirit who helps us in our weakness (Rom 8:26), gives us the strength to trust in God's promise of a new creation. The yearning of the Spirit within our hearts is the first fruits of this new creation and will gradually fill our spirits and spill out into the other anthropological dimensions of our lives. When seen in this light, the moral life becomes the way in which the Spirit helps us to live the Gospel on increasingly deeper and deeper levels of consciousness.[24]

Conclusion

No longer can the Christian life be artificially divided into the way of the law and the way of perfection. Precept and counsel, commandment and beatitude, virtue and gift are all bound together in an integral, inseparable unity. If moral theology is to give more emphasis to the role of the *Holy* Spirit, it must first retrieve its lost ties with the inner movements of the *human* spirit—the place within the person where the

[23] For the interplay of Christian spirituality with other religions, see Kosuke Koyama, "Interplay with Other Religions," *The Study of Spirituality,* 554–61. For Christian mysticism in dialogue with the religions of Asia and the resulting ethical implications, see Johnston, *Mystical Theology,* 120–54, 326–64.

[24] For the healing and elevating role of the Spirit, see Aquinas, *Summa Theologiae* I-II q.110 a.1 resp; q.113 a.2 resp. For the role of the Spirit in the moral life, see Pinckaers, *The Sources of Christian Ethics,* 177–82; Pinckaers, "L'instinct et l'Esprit au coeur de l'éthique chrétienne," 213–23.

divine and human meet. Only by including this neglected anthropological dimension in moral theological reflection will the human perspective of those concerned be broad enough to allow for a proper
discernment of the divine.[25]

The future orientation of Catholic moral theology will depend, to a
large degree, on how its spokespersons—both magisterial and profes-
sorial—construe (perhaps one should say "reconstrue") the relationship between rationality and spirituality. Reintegrating these key
aspects of the tradition would have two very important theological and
institutional effects. On the one hand, moral decision-making would
evidence a notable swing toward prayer and spiritual discernment in
helping to solve the dilemmas of conscience that arise among the faithful. This marked "spiritual turn" would move Catholic moral theology
away from its present fascination with the problem-solving machina-
tions of quandry ethics to an embracive relational paradigm rooted in
the divine-human encounter. Bishops and theologians, on the other
hand, would move away from their all too often adversarial way of
relating to a more collaborative, mutually-supportive stance. The
changed dynamics would bring to the fore the importance of rooting
moral theological reflection in the fullness of human experience (i.e.,
body, soul, *and* spirit), while at the same time highlighting the complementary ways in which the magisterium and Church theologians eluci-
date the tradition.

What is the future of moral theology? For the moment, let it simply
be said that, while the moral theology of the future will invariably include many things, it cannot afford to exclude or marginalize "the life
of the Spirit." In the present context, the latter phrase refers to rational
theological reflection rooted in a profound awareness of the human
spirit as it opens itself up to God's Spirit and allows the Word of God to
take shape and utter itself, however softly, within the confines of the
limited words and deeds by which we construct our human experience. Such a Word, however spoken, would resonate with authority
and not return in vain.

---

[25] For recent treatments of the relationship between the Holy Spirit and moral the-
ology, see Philip S. Keane, "The Role of the Holy Spirit in Contemporary Moral
Theology," *Catholic Theological Society of America: Proceedings of the Fifty-first Annual
Convention* (1996), ed. Judith A. Dwyer (New York: St. John's University, 1996)
97–113; Nonna Verna Harrison, "The Holy Spirit and Ethics: A Response to Philip
S. Keane, *CTSA Proceedings of the Fifty-first Annual Convention,* 114–19; James P.
Hanigan, "Conscience and the Holy Spirit," *CTSA Proceedings of the Fifty-first
Annual Convention,* 227–46; Dennis J. Billy, "The Person of the Holy Spirit as the
Source of the Christian Moral Life," *Studia Moralia* 36 (1998) 325–59.

Chapter Three

Listening, Prayer, and Conscience Formation

"If you want spiritual health, listen to your conscience, do all it tells you, and you will benefit."[1] This saying from *The Philokalia* reminds us that listening is an important skill for growth in the spiritual moral life. With it, we come to a deeper knowledge of ourselves and of our responsibilities before God and others. Without it, we lose sight of the constant inner dialogue that accompanies us at every step of our journey to fulfillment. In previous chapters, we examined the historical contours of the relationship between prayer and conscience in the Western Christian tradition and explored the connection between spirit and reason, two very important (and closely related) dimensions of human experience. In this chapter we will present a theology of listening. In it, we will set forth a vision of obedience understood as rapt listening, a listening that trains the heart to hear the truth. The truth is both propositional and personal for the Christian. The person of Jesus Christ, who is the way, the truth, and the life, embodies both the content of truth and its personal reality. Further, we understand this virtue of listening to be an aspect of the virtue of prudence. Prudence can be seen as the overall guiding virtue of moral living. Simply put, listening is the way prudence manifests itself in persons who respect conscience and also pray.

[1] *The Philokalia: The Complete Text*, trans. G.E.H. Palmer, Philip Sherrard, Kallistos Ware, vol. 1 (Boston: Faber and Faber, 1979) 115.

Listening in the Context of Christian Identity

For the Christian there is only a Christian ethic, not a philosophical ethic or a cultural ethic but only the kind of thinking about right and wrong that is born out of one's own mind sharing in the mind of Christ. Certainly the Christian ethic can be open to all that is true in other community ethics but first and foremost in Christian conscience formation the believer needs to attend to the sources of his or her baptismal identity. This baptismal identity is one that plunges the believer into a new reality of life in the Spirit. It is a life that does not jettison reason and affection but one that has come to utilize those powers as bathed in the virtues of faith, hope and love. In the commitment of the Christian life as lived in and through vocation, service, education and worship the believer endeavors to become vulnerable to the sanctifying actions of the Holy Spirit.

It is holiness that truly beckons the Christian. In baptism the desire and the means to fulfill the desire for "divinization" are initiated. Divinization, or holiness, is the state of participating in the divine nature. This sharing in the divine nature is never fully accomplished before death as we are always in need of some purification of sin. Whereas many of us would see the saintly persons we may know as being completely one with God, the saintly themselves are aware of possessing a certain level of sin. In them, however, we see what we long to be, open to God, and eager to receive grace, goodness, and conversion.

We long to be in communion with God. Being good and choosing rightly attract the Christian because in virtuous living one invites and cooperates with the divine gift of holiness. The moral virtues, imbued with charity, direct us to our ultimate happiness by uniting us to God. For the believer, intimacy with God is the true goal of being good. This goal may not always be in the forefront of consciousness with each act born of virtue, but it is the quiet goal of all who seek to live out the goodness that moral virtue contains. As we mentioned above in chapter two, our final end has important ramifications for how we live our lives.

And so, the believer who seeks to live the moral life is not artificially segmented into a religious person and a moral person; rather, these two distinct realities coalesce in the one person who is the Christian. Being good and loving the Source of that goodness is the content of the Christian moral life. This life of moral goodness and devotion to God is expressed most clearly in the relation between conscience and prayer. The conscience, the heart of the moral life, and prayer, the center of devotion to God, conspire to assist the believer to come into deeper union with all that is good and holy.

This union between conscience and prayer can best be known through developing the virtue of listening. It is in listening that one inclines the "heart" to the object of love, to the beloved who speaks the truth. For many of us the desire to listen has to develop over time, as we do not always want to hear the truth about ourselves whether spoken by beloved friend or an enemy. Of course, having the truth spoken by a friend is more palatable, and can also insure that it is spoken not in order to destroy but, rather, to build up. Ultimately, however, it is Christ, the beloved, who speaks the truth. Christ is beloved in the sense that he is the bearer of truth regarding our human condition and to listen to him is to listen to our heart's desire—attaining a life in fidelity to human dignity. Also, we love Christ because he is the fulfillment of our deepest desire—the union of the human with the divine. In this union we are completed in the very source of our existence and come to know the fruits of peace and charity. We love Christ because he is, qualitatively speaking, who we want to be, who we are destined to be—persons in union with God. In union with Christ we become more ourselves than we have ever been before. Listening to him will cost us our egos but it will not cost us our very selves. In listening to Christ we will come to fulfillment, as he is the fulfillment of all humanity in God. In listening to Christ we are listening to our deepest identity as human persons—as those who strive for moral goodness and unity with God. This unity of goodness and divinity is for us holiness and for Christ his rightful glory.

John Henry Newman once stated a truth relevant to our present study: "Is not holiness the result of many patient, repeated efforts after obedience, gradually working on us, and first modifying and then changing our hearts."[2] Obedience has a harsh sound to many in Western culture today. Authentic obedience is not about the fearful response to an abusive or tyrannical authority. Authentic obedience is the stance of one who listens intently for and to the truth. The more we grow in virtue the more we want to be obedient to the truth because we love it. Analogically speaking, love would be the positive reason the word "obey" was placed in some wedding vows in the past. The spouses promised to listen to one another because they love one another, not because one is inferior and the other superior. Whether or not the word "obey" is formally in the vows today, married persons know that the truth of promising to listen to one's spouse is absolutely vital if loving union is to be achieved. The absence of the virtue of listening in many marriages is a reason why they fail. If this is not true why else would communication skills be the prime discipline marriage counselors try

---

[2] John Henry Newman, "Holiness Necessary for Future Blessedness," *Parochial and Plain Sermons*, vol. 1 (London: Longmans, Green, & Co., 1900) 11.

to impart to their client couples? To become holy one has to learn to listen to God. This listening affects our character over time and thus Newman can say that obedience changes our hearts.

Listening to God and to the truth about our moral lives works its way into our dispositions and attitudes in such a way that over time listening to God simply becomes who one is. I am one who listens, one who is obedient to what he loves. This conversion to a life of listening is normally accomplished in small steps. Most of us have grown to incline the ear to what is true and good over time, sometimes imperceptibly so. Once a religious or moral conversion begins a person may well perceive that in the past he had given the ear of his heart to authorities and loves previously unnamed but definitely real. In the light of Christ and the moral truth the superficial aspects of previous loves and authorities becomes clear. One laments, "how could I have given myself to such a one for so long?" Listening to objects of love or authority is not an option. We all do it as matter of course. To consciously change what or whom we listen to does oftentimes cause some pain within us. The pain caused is due to the nature of listening.

When one listens, the conscience, the spiritual center of thought and feeling, is molded according to the object of our listening. When we divert our listening from previous objects to new centers of devotion, love and attention there can be a "tearing away" that is noticeable. This is why people reverse apparent conversions on occasion. When setting out to listen to new sources of meaning we may find it difficult to incline the ear toward a different object of love or meaning. This pain makes some people return to the previous object of obedience. This phenomenon is as old as the Exodus story (Exod 16:1ff) and the characters therein who wanted to go back to slavery once the pain of the desert became too intense. Our conversions away from false realities and teachers will be accomplished through little steps within the ordinariness of our days. *Gradually* letting go of inadequate objects of love appears as the most normal course for persons embarking on the journey of moral conversion. Some persons, however, are asked to sever ties to sources of immorality quickly and absolutely depending upon the perversity of the source's influence.

Christian Identity and Conscience Formation

In Catholic moral living the notion of listening to what is true has to be seen within a context of the many realities impinging upon a person and community. Prime among these realities is the interplay between grace and sin. One cannot naively say that all a person has to do is intently listen to religious sources and the moral truth will be known and executed. Vices, such as sloth, pride, and self-deception can cloud one's ability to listen objectively and contextually. In the present time *contextual* listening is most urgent. By this we mean that one listens for and to moral truth out of an explicitly Christian context and identity. The baptismal identity has all too often been muted in Western culture, simply residing in the background of decision-making. This muting of the religious identity during moral decision-making removes the chosen act from the context of one's real life as a Christian. Is one or is one not a Christian? If one is a Christian, this identity *is* our reality and from out of this identity moral decisions ought to flow. There is no "place" one can go and be completely objective or neutral.[3] In fact neutrality does not serve the goal of overcoming pride, sloth or self-deception. Only commitment to the sources of Christian life can do that for the disciple. In one's commitment to a life of faith, hope and love the Christian's identity is clarified, focused and known. Recall how in chapter one we noted the influence of William of Ockham on the eventual separation of faith from reason and will. Conscience simply came to be seen as reason bowing to law. Prayer and one's Christian devotion then had very little to do with moral decision-making.

For the Christian to listen for Christ's truth in the church, and for vestiges of Christ in the culture, is the normal work of the evangelized conscience.[4] To have a religiously formed and sensitive conscience is neither extraneous nor artificial; it is simply to be who one is before God. It is only when the conscience has been formed by listening to sources devoid of Christian dignity or content that the conscience and its judgments regarding truth appear too burdensome.

This is not to say that what the conscience judges to be morally true will be easy to do; it will call upon all our courage to obey, but listening itself to the judgment of conscience will *not* be a struggle—we will want to listen. The Christian will want to know what is true and good and beautiful. The lives of the saints indicate that even the struggle to "do" the truth known by conscience becomes less and less of a struggle over years of virtuous living. This ease of doing the truth does not mean temptation is totally eradicated or intellectual confusion cannot exist, but it does testify to the fact that over years of living the virtues the moral life becomes "a light burden" (Matt 11:30).

---

[3] Andrew Dell'Olio, "God, The Self, and The Ethic of Virtue," *Philosophy and Theology* 11:1 (1998) 47–69.

[4] James Keating, "Evangelizing Conscience" *Pro Ecclesia* 8:4 (1999) 475–87.

Furthermore, listening to the truth does not necessarily create rigid or authoritarian believers and leaders. When persons practice the virtue of listening to God and conscience and in turn teach others to do the same they transmit the faith humbly and gratefully because they know better than most that moral truth is received as grace.

Here is where fruitful cooperation between theologian and magisterium can occur as both seek to know the truth in the tensions of their relationships, and as thinking persons, within the *promise* of Christ's abiding presence.

Passing on the moral teachings of the church has very little to do with "being right" in judgmental fashion but everything to do with "being righteous." To be righteous means that one who comes to know what is good does so from out of the depth of his or her relation with God. In following this moral path, the relationship with God is confirmed, and, alternately, one knows more deeply what is morally good in this union with God. This is righteousness. It gives birth to humility and gratitude since one knows that he or she would be nothing without grace—without the self-donation of God in Christ to human persons.

From within this graced relationship we come to see what is morally good not in order to judge others before God but in order to know God better ourselves.[5] Moral living is not a prize bestowed upon those who "grin and bear it" but rather a life that flows out of a state of being in love with God, expressed through dispositions and activities congruent with that love relationship. The "reward" for being good and choosing rightly is simply intimacy with God, the author of all goodness. In this way the life of moral goodness is a dim foretaste of heaven, thus yielding happiness.

A Creative Tension

We are concerned in this book with the integration of prayer and conscience simply as a specification of that most ancient of tension-filled realities—divinity and humanity, grace and nature, sacred and secular. Only in the mystery of Christ are these poles held in perfect creative tension without confusion or denigration of one or the other pole. Both the secular and the sacred can be vehicles for the completion of one or the other—prayer can expand to include the goodness of all creation, and moral behavior can expand to include its ultimate origin in God's own goodness and not simply the goodness of human per-

---

[5] Of course, using a Spirit-inspired reason, one can judge the objective immorality of others' acts. This is manifestly true or else we would never be able to legislate civil order.

sons. The sacred and secular, prayer and conscience are not ultimately opposed or separate but in Christ united and integrated. This integration is our ultimate hope and it is why we desire to follow the truth in conscience and adore the One who authors all moral truth.

The life of Christ provides a perfect image of the listening heart—conscience—as he fastened it upon every word from the Father. St. John Eudes, who authored the first Mass in honor of the Sacred Heart of Jesus, chose as his theme for this mass the conversion of the sinner away from evil through the devotion to Christ and his virtues. The essential virtue of Christ presented in this liturgy is that of Jesus listening to his Father's voice and sharing the fruit of that listening and intimacy with his disciples. "I have told you everything I have heard from my Father" (John 15:15).[6] The listening done by Christ, however, was not simply an act of attending to the oral delivery of fascinating information. It was a listening oriented toward action. In the Letter of James we read this: "Be doers of the word and not hearers only, deluding yourselves. For if anyone is a hearer of the word and not a doer, he is like a man who looks at his own face in a mirror . . . then goes off and promptly forgets what he looked like" (Jas 1:22-24). Newman describes this kind of listening that leads to action as one that springs from faith. Through and in faith any knowledge gained by listening can be utilized for the spiritual formation of the person. It is to this kind of listening that one can attach the description obedience. Obedience is a listening unto action. Obedience is a kind of knowing that costs and exacts a certain level of self-sacrifice with it. Obeying is a readied, eager listening to what is true. The truth bids one to enact it despite any pain caused to the selfish ego. In this way listening is an ascetical practice. Newman is prophetically harsh in his description of those who reduce knowledge to listening without action. "And any one here present who falls short of this, that is, who thinks it enough to come to church to *learn* God's will, but does not bear in mind to do it in his daily conduct, . . . he is a fool in [God's] sight, who maketh the wisdom of this world foolishness."[7]

Listening as an Expression of Prudence

It is not simply listening that assists in the proper formation of conscience. As noted above one must be ready to enact the truth one has

---

[6] See James Keating, "Listening to Christ's Heart: Moral Theology and Spirituality in Dialogue," *Milltown Studies* 39 (Summer 1997) 59.

[7] Newman, "Knowledge of God's Will Without Obedience," *Parochial and Plain Sermons*, vol. 1, 34.

heard. This kind of readiness needs to be instilled through a life of virtue within a community of virtue. One needs courage to overcome any fear that is generated from the ruling selfish ego in order to enact the truth one hears in prayer, reading or counsel. Over some time of cooperating with the moral truth persons will attain a tolerable level of fear, one that can be more easily conquered through prayer or even simple willing, but novices in the spiritual moral life will struggle more mightily to overcome the influence of self-interest and other vices.

There are many expressions of prudence, but a very important expression would be found in the act of rapt listening. Listening to the truth is impossible in any conscience development without the virtue of prudence and its reality of guiding one to appropriate formation sources, and then to morally good actions.[8] Prudence is knowledge of the correct means to the correct ends of our actions. Prudence is a practical virtue that enables us to implement correct means to achieve the rational ends of our actions. To be rash is to act on impulse; to be prudent is to act on sure knowledge based upon a sound grasp of many moral factors including the dignity of the human person, our baptism in Christ, our church membership. The prudent person can make moral decisions with greater ease but it is usually only after a complex reasoning and affective process of formation that such facility in ethical knowledge emerges.

By complex reasoning and affective formation we do not mean to imply that only the learned person or schooled person can achieve the necessary prudence for the Christian ethical life. Yes, one must be schooled in the virtues and in holiness and in the disciplines of discipleship but moral knowledge is not always connected to formal education. We are all familiar with saints who could "sense" that something was morally wrong but could not really articulate why it was so, nor could they give an eloquent defense in favor of moral goodness; rather, they just knew that their own or someone else's judgment was in error. This way of sensing moral error and, alternately, moral truth is not an extreme exception in Catholic moral living but in fact the norm to be expected after years of formation in virtuous living, worship, prayer, devotion and study. It is an exercise in connatural knowledge, knowledge born of love and attention to the good and true. "Rational deliberation is necessary but not sufficient in discovering what is moral, not by knowledge alone, but by the full flower of knowledge, love, is the moral good to be fully engaged and lived. Discursive knowledge gives some little help in dealing with life's challenges and

[8] Daniel Nelson, *The Priority of Prudence* (University Park, Penn.: Pennsylvania State University Press, 1992); Josef Pieper, *Prudence* (New York: Pantheon, 1959).

decisions. The knowledge that truly remains is intimacy with God."[9] Andrew Tallon articulates well the role of connatural knowing in moral life. "Connatural knowing and loving are not the exceptions, the back up system as it were, for when discursive, conceptual knowledge and deliberative freedom fail . . . but just the opposite: it is when discernment of spirits by affective connaturality in one's personal situation fails (when you 'just don't have it in you') that you then must fall back by default on reasoning discursively from general principles."[10] While affective connaturality appears as the fruit of virtuous living this is not to imply that discursive reasoning is to be willfully jettisoned for some lone affective route to moral truth. Affective connaturality is fruit and gift emerging after years of discursive reasoning and virtuous living.

Through years of listening to the fullness of Christian life, a life that includes personal experience, prayer, service, worship, study, conversion, one takes on a listening heart. This kind of heart encompasses a stance of humility and docility. Again these virtues are not the passive, weak attitudes that many fear they are. One who is humble and docile lives in the truth; I am incomplete, I do not know it all, I have to look to others in the community to assist my understanding of what is morally good. This is not weakness but a life of strength lived out of knowing the truth about oneself and about how one comes to know and do moral behavior.

To listen in humility and with docility to and for the moral truth is a disposition that has gotten many Catholics killed. Martyrdom is a suffering born out of one's love for the truth. Martyrdom can be seen as a paradigm for all faithful listening to the truth that the conscience detects. Within the essence of martyrdom is the relinquishing of one form of life for the hope and promise of another, one not fully seen but glimpsed by the knowledge one has through faith, truth and goodness. Truly listening to the truth and acting upon it takes a courage gained only within a deep trust in the promises of Christ. Both prudence and courage cooperate within the Christian martyr to yield moral action that bespeaks a deeper locus of origin in God. In living a life of faith, truth and goodness a person begins to breathe within these virtues and dwell within the reality they reveal. This revelation is one that points the martyr beyond this present moment of self-interest and current concerns to offer his or her life up for the ultimate value of living truthfully in God. This is the summit of human fidelity

[9] Karl Rahner, *Prayers for a Lifetime*, ed. Albert Raffelt (New York: Crossroad, 1987) 17.

[10] Andrew Tallon, "The Heart in Rahner's Philosophy of Mysticism," *Theological Studies* 53 (1992) 711.

and the community rightly looks to the martyr as one to admire and if possible, emulate.

The moral martyrdom of a person who listens to conscience shares many of the same virtues, as the martyr who gives over his or her life to death. For the moral martyr, is willing to listen to the moral truth even at the cost of his or her ego. Those who struggle to live the spiritual moral life know that this struggle is near the core of daily living. Of course one does not feel such struggle as a conscious battle every moment, that would be maddening, but the one who comes closer and closer to moral goodness in Christ can detect this struggle always present just beneath the surface of daily dispositions and choices.

The martyrdom of moral living is a killing of selfishness not the self. It may appear that such strong language as "killing" is not appropriate for the experience of moral fidelity. In the initial stages of listening to conscience, however, the struggle to assent to truth can be so intense that it does feel like something inside of us is dying. And at least spiritually, there is a real death going on, it is a death to selfishness and vice. So we do not think it is such a stretch of the imagination or simply a metaphor to say that the listening of conscience brings about martyrdom. The ego is offered up so that the fullness of truth about the self can become manifest in actions on behalf of moral goodness. Listening costs.

Talking Too Much: The Call for Silence

When one listens there is the necessary implication of the presence of a speaker, a source to whom a person is attending. As Pope Paul VI noted, however, the contemporary person is "sated by talk" and often "tired of listening and, what is worse, impervious to words. . . . The fatigue produced these days by so much empty talk . . . must not however diminish the permanent power of the word, or cause a loss of confidence in it."[11] If we live in a talk-filled world the remedy for the kind of fatigue Paul VI is alluding to here is the call to silence. In a paradoxical way allowing oneself to sit in silence prepares one better to receive words that bear the truth. One of the authors of this book was observing the teaching method of a kindergarten teacher one day. He noticed that whenever the class would get too noisy and agitated the teacher would lower her voice to a whisper and even at times simply go silent. If she went silent the class would continue to chatter and be

[11] Paul VI, Pope, *Evangelii Nuntiandi* (On Evangelization in the Modern World) (Washington, D.C.: United States Catholic Conference, 1976) 42.

busy for a minute or two and then slowly and imperceptibly the silence of the teacher would envelop the students in silence as well. A wave of silence would gently fill the room and encompass everyone. Out of this silence the teacher would speak again and give new information or directions that the students actually heard and enacted.

In the same manner, if we allow silence to envelop us during times of meditation or prayer we may learn to hear the voice of the teacher, Christ. We are invited to train the heart to listen to the still small voice of God. Walter Wangerin has identified three traditional areas within which we can first grow silent and then listen for the truth and for God.

First, he notes that almsgiving as a way of life helps us to focus our attention upon others in need and move us out into the world. If we can silence our own unrelenting neediness and self-preoccupation for a moment the needs of others may get a hearing within our hearts and so give space for charity to form within us as a permanent disposition.[12]

Second, Wangerin mentions the need for fasting. Fasting disciplines the soul privately and prepares a person to welcome the truth about his or her interdependency upon others and dependency upon God. Fasting is not to be seen simply as a denial of food to self but as a denial of any word or action that may inhibit the heart from attending to God and the needs of others.

Third, prayer is seen to be the act of seeking the sacred and pondering it. As we noted above in chapter one, prayer is keeping company with God. In all three of these disciplines we seek to clear a space and wait to hear the voice of God. "To hear the voice of God at all requires preparation of the soul. . . . Since the soul is the inner ear by which we hear the Spirit in intimate conversation, we must regularly clear it out, purge it of sin and of the self that deafens it."[13] The silence that prepares a person to listen more readily is the silence that precedes communion with another. This is a unique kind of silence different from its opposite kind known in the fruits of selfish or isolated living. Wangerin notes the following about this negative kind of silence. "[In sin] the heavens will seem vastly silent to us, and all the world a lonely place—not because God is not talking, but rather because we cannot hear his voice."[14] We become more and more self-enclosed through sin and hence can only come to hear our own voice; God's voice becomes silenced. This kind of silence is the ominous sign of alienation and lonely confusion whereas the waiting silence previously described holds the promise of imminent communion with truth and of one's beloved. This

---

[12] Walter Wangerin, *Whole Prayer* (Grand Rapids: Zondervan, 1998) 177.
[13] Wangerin, *Whole Prayer*, 190.
[14] Wangerin, *Whole Prayer*, 191.

waiting silence is akin to the expectation known by pregnant women as they anticipate in the quiet of pregnancy the new life that will soon fill their lives. And as with the birth of children we know that welcoming the new life that God may bring will be both exhilarating and trying. But overall one expects that welcoming new life in all its forms will lead to happiness.

Re-Evangelization:
Listening Anew to the One We Love

To know happiness through moral and religious conversion we need to know that we can trust the sources to which we have listened. The key to moral growth is located in identifying what or whom we trust in sufficiently to listen to and to have faith in. If it has not been God to whom we have given this trust we know through the promises of Scripture that God is always willing to call out again to those who have not listened (Zech 1:3; Mal 3:7), to those who have hardened their hearts to his word. Of course this call must be responded to and in time a refusal to listen to God can define a person as such. This hardening of the heart is akin to the very common situation wherein people *hear* what others have to say but really do not *listen*.

In current Western culture many have heard the Gospel preached but the perennial question is posed: Have they listened to it and enacted it? Some persons hear the Gospel with the same listless disposition that a grandson might hold toward hearing the stories his grandfather has shared with him over and over again. When we are young we are eager to hear the stories again and again, but then we come into adolescence and the re-told stories are received only wearily. We begin to half-listen or politely listen but refuse to commune with the narrative or the story-teller. We are bored with the same old tales. Why is this? Might it be that we have lost touch with the storyteller, we are less interested in his life and so become ready to dismiss his tales as irrelevant? Of course, repetition can have a naturally boring quality to it, but this is acutely felt only if we have no relationship to the stories or the narrator. In some ways Christians can become alienated from the stories of their own identity just like a grandson can drift from his grandfather's circle of influence or intimacy. (It is also possible that the grandfather has contributed to the problem by not listening to the grandson's needs or stories either.) When this alienation happens between God and his people the call goes out in the church for re-evangelization.

Christ has not called us to "politely listen" or simply endure the Gospel but rather to make it our food (John 4:34, 6:27). As Christians we are to *live* off of the Gospel, as Christ lived off every word that came from his Father. Christ's whole disposition was one of eager listening to the Father. The Letter to the Hebrews notes that our very salvation is linked to our ability to listen to Christ (Heb 5:9). Through what Paul called the "obedience of faith" the Christian works out his or her salvation within a continual communion with God in Christ. This obedience of faith is the disposition that restores us to our correct relationship with God as opposed to our tendency to choose sin.[15]

Regarding sin, Columba Stewart has noted that obedience, or rapt listening to God, at its "basic level rejects the futility of isolation, left to ourselves we can do little but despair."[16] For Stewart, obedience is seen to be essentially a conversation, the most fundamental one being between oneself and God. This conversational model of obedience lends itself well to the Psalmist's plea, "If today you hear his voice harden not your heart" (Ps 95:8). The reality of a life lived without obedience to God descending into profound isolation and despair is echoed in the writings of Jean Pierre de Caussade. Moreover, for Cassaude the despair we experience is also the ignition for a new life in faith:

> The truly spiritual have very different feelings and act very differently. Strongly imbued with their nothingness, with both their misery and their weakness, they are neither discouraged nor devastated nor even surprised by their relapses. From them they learn to know themselves better, to humble themselves . . . and to even despair of themselves fully, in order to place their confidence exclusively in God alone and to wait for no more than his goodness.[17]

The result of listening to God is profound humility. The one who listens to God is not morally perfect and he or she knows it. One does, however, revere the kind of moral living that comes from such an intimate relationship with God and he or she never ceases to desire it or beg God for his mercy when there is a failure to adhere to the truth. A humility about oneself, a true assessment of one's state before objective moral truth, gives rise to compassion for the sinner not a judgmental distancing of the self from the "impure." The one who is obedient knows that his or her graduated "success" in the moral life depends not on moral athleticism but simply a deep disposition to receive the gift of salvation from within a living relationship to God in Christ.

[15] Donald Garlington, *Faith, Obedience and Perseverance* (Tubingen: J.C.B. Mohr, 1994) 104.

[16] Columba Stewart, *Prayer and Community* (Maryknoll, N.Y.: Orbis, 1998) 54.

[17] Jean Pierre de Caussade, *A Treatise on Prayer from the Heart* (St. Louis: Institute of Jesuit Sources, 1998) 130.

A further fruit of listening to God, beyond humility, is the virtue of purity of heart. This purity abides in the heart's interior silence, admiration and love of God. The one who listens strives to act out of the love of God and for the love of what God loves. Caussade notes that those who are pure of heart become so as they spend more and more time thinking about God. In the light of this they realize that if one thinks of God, God will think *of* that person, and if one thinks like God, God will think *for* that person.[18] This kind of language is frightening to westerners who hold on to themselves "for dear life" in an effort to control all and preserve themselves from some dreaded annihilation in communion with others. Those, like the saints among us, who are on the way toward full union with the divine, neither fear nor dread that union; they know that within that union is their only hope of preserving and knowing the self, not its eradication. So, says the saint, "I will leave space for you to think of me and I will think virtuously as you do, so that you, O God, will fill my mind with your wisdom." The saint knows that all have sinned and fallen short of the glory of God (Rom 3:23) and so acknowledging the need to listen to God and to even long for the day when God will fill one's mind with his wisdom is simply to live in reality. As Stewart teaches, "Humility is both the companion and fruit of someone who wants to grow in obedience. This is so because humility is the mode of being of someone who hears and takes to heart every reminder of dependence on God alone."[19]

This stance of humble listening to God is best exercised throughout the day because one never knows when God will approach through creation in grace. Only the vulnerable in heart can discern the often subtle divine voice speaking to us out of the ordinary circumstances of daily routines. For example, there was a businessman who out of necessity stayed home one day to care for his young child of six months. The man's wife had to go to work on an unscheduled day and so the husband was pressed into child-care service. Since he had many projects and deadlines looming at work he *reluctantly* agreed to stay home

---

[18] Caussade *Treatise on Prayer from the Heart*, 145, note 38, where Caussade quotes St. Catherine of Siena. This dependency feature of life in God is not to be arrogantly snatched from its proper religious context and used by those in political or social positions of power to justify any oppression of the poor or vulnerable. The language of obedience, humility, and service is one that rightly belongs to the theological realm and not the political, per se. Unlike one's relationship to God, obedience to earthly authority "does not subject the one who obeys to the person in authority as such but [obedience to authority] integrates the one who obeys to the end and good of a particular society [e.g., economics, political, ecclesial]. See Karl Rahner et al., *Obedience and the Church* (Washington, D.C.: Corpus Books, 1968) 4.

[19] Stewart, *Prayer and Community*, 56.

that day. While ruminating over his frustrated workday he decided to take his baby out for a walk in the carriage. As he rounded a corner in his neighborhood a jogger ran by and then stopped to turn around and look at the baby, saying to the man, "You have the best job in the world, you know that?" and then ran off. The father was dumbfounded and began to reassess what was really important in his life and why he possessed such a negative disposition toward home and family life. Certainly this man could have hardened his heart against the word from the jogger but instead he listened, he was humble enough to question his own values and motives and make room for a word beyond his own.

Making room to receive a word beyond one's own is what obedience is all about. It is a virtue that broadens the narrow confines of the worlds we have made in order to feel safe or controlling. God's word, however, always comes in from beyond, even when it is acknowledged deep within our conscience. To become obedient, to faithfully listen for the truth, is the way to become one who attends to a fuller reality than simply what the pattern of controllable habits has created in our daily choosing. We ought to practice the presence of God because God touches the vulnerable and humble through many sources in his creation, and so closing our hearts to disregard some sources as not worthy of listening to may be too hasty a judgment. No source is to be spurned—but the content of the message must be properly *discerned*. Here again prudence dictates that not all words "beyond one's own" are simply acceptable due to their origin in another. What guides the believer's listening is his or her dignity as a disciple. This dignity is known and embraced primarily by the full engagement one gives to the *Christian* life. Our engagement of Scripture, participation in worship and catechesis, and service to the poor, if approached with the desire to be affected by God who is Truth, is the best formation of discernment capability. The intensity of a full Christian life gives one a character bent on rightfully apprehending the good from whatever source it comes and rejecting evil no matter what authority espouses it. This capacity *is* "the freedom of the children of God" (Rom 8:21) and paradoxically can be known only in obedience to the truth. We fear the virtue of obedience because we fear what is outside and beyond what we presently know as our reality. God calls us to listen in prayer and in conscience because it is here, in the deepest part of our heart that the divine intimacy transforms us into truly moral persons. By listening to God we become friends with God and with our neighbors and ourselves. It is dis-obedience that alienates and enslaves, not obedience. When a married couple argues, the argument is never resolved if one or the other blurts out in anger, "You are not listening to me." There can be no understanding, no communion, and no real order without the humble stance of listening. This is the great insight of psychological therapy. Therapists oftentimes simply listen so that the client can hear himself, and maybe for the first time listen to himself about the truth regarding his emotions and life. In an environment of listening the client is brought to some peace and reconciliation with himself. In Christian moral living the virtue of listening, and enacting what one has heard, bestows peace upon the explicit relationship between persons and God, and not simply the self.

Conclusion

Obedience, or rapt listening, is a virtue ripe for revisiting in our day. Not that there needs to be any more obedience—Western culture is filled with obedient persons who attend to each and every word uttered by political, media, fashion, and entertainment sources. We need a more discerning listening, one that springs not from what is only current but from the depths of our enduring identity as having died to sin so as to live in Christ. We spend our days hidden with Christ in God (Col 3:3). It will be the virtue of prudence that guides and directs the person aware of his Christian identity to discern more accurately worthy sources of conscience formation. Practicing the virtue of prudence in the context of one's baptismal identity regenerates the individual to choose the correct means and ends of behavior that are in accord with the dignity of the baptized life. Listening to influential sources out of love or necessity is inescapable; what is within one's free choice is to whom or what we attend. What is the source of truth for the Christian, upon whom should we train our hearts to listen? Abuse by those in authority regarding the obligation to obey is to be condemned but so also is the trend to jettison rigorous analysis of the worth of current cultural and political sources to whom we give, at times, unquestioning obedience. And further, it is not the virtue of obedience per se that is the weak link in a Christian moral-spiritual life, it is the lack of effort or sloth exhibited in discerning legitimate founts of life from which to drink.[20]

---

[20] Kenneth Himes, "Conscience and Sloth," *Spirituality and Moral Theology,* ed. James Keating (Mahwah, N.J.: Paulist Press, 2000).

Chapter Four

Prayer and Conscience: Openness to the Truth in Christ

"True words from a pure conscience betoken unfeigned love."[1] These words from *The Philokalia* remind us of the close connection between truth and love. For the Christian, openness to the Truth finds its fulfillment in a personal relationship with Christ. This relationship is a friendship of benevolent and mutual indwelling, which provides the context for all else that happens in the spiritual moral life. In the last chapter we presented the virtue of listening as key to the theological endeavor of unifying prayer and conscience. The obvious question that remains is, "To whom do we listen and how does one develop the skills and habits of listening in a formative way?" In this chapter, we will examine some of the key elements involved in what is typically referred to as "putting on the mind of Christ" (1 Cor.2:16).

Attention Toward Christ

If the conscience is to be formed according to the full dignity of the Christian person as one who is taking on the mind of Christ and not simply the mind of the current popular or political culture then such a formation has to be explicit and guided. The explicit focus of Christian conscience formation is found in the community's commitment to attend to Christ. This attention is expressed in myriad ways but has its

---

[1] *The Philokalia: The Complete Text*, trans. G.E.H. Palmer, Philip Sherrard, Kallistos Ware, vol. 2 (Boston: Faber and Faber, 1979) 307.

most explicit locus in the Eucharist and in a person's or community's service to the poor. The formation of a Christian conscience is not to be exclusively discursive or cerebral. Certainly being good and choosing rightly is about the mind judging right from wrong but moral living has its emphasis upon becoming good not simply being "smart." By all means one is called to reach his or her own intellectual potential but intelligence in itself is no guarantee of the ultimate moral goal of Christianity—a holiness founded upon and within a desired moral goodness. And being good involves being in a relationship of Love with God in Christ. For the Christian conscience the fullness of the person, in spirit, mind, and body develops an openness to the *presence* of the true and good and holy. This openness toward these realities is concretized in one's openness toward Christ, as the ultimate embodiment of these qualities. In times of urgency or during childhood one may simply resort to following rules in the moral life but over the long run of Christian maturation it is the work of paying attention to Christ that truly seals the contents of one's conscience. Rules are not useless nor is their application wrong, it is simply that they are not sufficient in some situations where a moral decision is called for.

This is true because over time Christ becomes the content of the conscience. "I no longer live not I but Christ lives in me" (Gal 2:20). This Christification of the person also becomes the hallmark of the person's character. One actually becomes a bearer of Christ. This transformation has been enabled through worship (Eucharist), Word, and charity (service to the poor). In fact we become good by attending to these sources because they are for us the "weak points" of creation through which God can more easily be encountered in his call to holiness. That is not to say that one must be fully aligned with Christ in body, mind and spirit before one can make an ethical decision or even pass on moral advice to others. It does, however, mean that one can only live explicitly 'in Christ' if he or she is open to the grace offered through baptism. The mind may not be fully aligned and the will and body may not be fully conformed to Christ but the spirit is yearning for completion in the Holy Spirit. Through such a desire persons begin to serve the moral good.

In this vision of the Christian moral life the human spirit reaching out for the Holy Spirit is key to growth in conscience and character. As we explicated in chapter two this spirit speaking to the Holy Spirit or a heart speaking to a heart[2] highlights the personalistic dimension of Christian ethics. Our spirit, our ability to reach beyond the self and commune with the divine, and God's will to initiate this desire and

---

[2] John Henry Newman, *Parochial and Plain Sermons,* vol. 5 (London: Longmans, Green & Co., 1902) 234.

then consummate it, contain the guiding dynamic for all Christian conscience formation. The spirit of an individual person can be taught by the Holy Spirit. The conscience can learn what is good from a life of devotion, worship and service. The need today, however, is to recover in persons an awareness of the ongoing formation of conscience at every moment of every day. Further, there is a need to foster a deeper respect for the skills of discerning (as will be discussed in chapter five) what one ought to allow to permeate the mind, what one ought to allow to affect the spirit and move the body.[3]

Conscience understood, as we noted above in chapter one, as "a knowing-with" grounds our deepest sense of the relevance of prayer to conscience. This knowing-with is a knowing with *Christ.* Since conversing with Christ in the Eucharist, the Scriptures, the lives of the saints and in service to the poor does not carry answers to every contemporary moral question, as we noted in chapter two, some were tempted to see a two-level world for Christian ethics: a devotional one and a deliberative one where law and reason play a part. In fact we will argue just the opposite, nothing is so able to penetrate the circumstantial and nuanced moments of categorical decisions as is the mind of the one who has allowed Christ to love him or her. In fact, for the Christian, knowing with Christ can assist him or her to penetrate the ordinary circumstances of living with and in virtue. Certainly law, or custom or majority vote cannot bring what the living Christian does to each moral decision: a mind and heart formed out of a profound relationship with Christ in the Eucharist, in service and in study. Law remains too removed, abstract and at times historically conditioned to apply to all situations.[4] The one to be trusted most in concrete situations calling for moral judgments when there are no clear-cut norms is the Christian moral virtuoso deliberating, if need be, or simply acting out of connatural knowledge. In other words, it is the living saint among us who best embodies the possibility of getting the moral answer to difficult questions. This is not to say there is a privileged or infallible charism given to saints, certainly persons with lesser characters can discern the truth if there is openness to discovering it. It is the saint however, who in his or her very *essence* is that person who *is* open to discover the truth in and through a relationship with Christ in the church.[5]

---

[3] See Anthony Ciorra and James Keating, *Moral Formation in the Parish* (New York: Alba House, 1998) 59–86.

[4] Certainly law is legitimate and can represent the truth where promulgated by governing bodies or majority vote. In fact, if more Christians would "vote" their faith-informed conscience, the social structures ideally might be more just.

[5] See Donna Orsuto, "The Saint as Moral Paradigm," *Spirituality and Morality,* ed. Dennis Billy and Donna Orsuto (Mahwah, N.J.: Paulist, 1996) 127–40.

The saint carries within his or her conscience the sources of an intimate encounter with Christ that has fed other saints over two thousand years: worship, prayer, service to the poor and catechesis. For the virtuous Christian there is no fear of solipsism because it has been his honor and desire to drink deeply from sources other than (simply) the self. In many cases it was sickness of the self that drove the saint to jettison the puny enclosed mind of an individual and submit that mind, spirit and body to deeper listening beyond the self in Christ. As Hans Urs Von Balthasar has noted, it is the rejection of the personal encounter with Christ in ethics that most assuredly gives rise to a twisted legalism. This legalism fosters an unending guilt that cannot be eradicated no matter how many new laws we create either to make ourselves feel better or re-structure society.[6]

Prayer, Conscience, and Christian Spirituality

Christian spirituality is that discipline which focuses upon the person of Christ in his concrete life as norm and thus, as Karl Rahner asserts, avoids any disintegration into a "theoretical morality."[7] Christian spirituality is Trinitarian and therefore dialogic. It is founded upon the belief that "God has communicated to humanity and that humans can respond. We are taken up into an open dialogue which includes the Father, Son, and Spirit. Jesus is the mediation between the Father and ourselves and thus delivers us to the Father."[8] The characteristic component of Christian spirituality is that the deepest meaning of human life is forever connected to the humanity of Jesus Christ. If an authentic Christian spirituality is to be articulated, this enduring bond with the human on the part of Christ's own humanity must be considered.

It is in a Trinitarian spirituality that we can see plainly the illusion of understanding prayer as an escape from the world. The Trinitarian reality of pouring oneself out for and in the world is the lodestar for any ethic which holds spirituality to be relevant in the discernment of good and moral evil. Authentic Christian prayer will open one up to the needs of the world just as the Father was open in the sending of Christ and through the perpetual enabling of our prayer in the Holy Spirit.

[6] Joseph Ratzinger, Heinz Schurmann, and Hans Urs von Balthasar, *Principles of a Christian Morality* (San Francisco: Ignatius Press, 1986) 92–95.

[7] Karl Rahner, *The Practice of Faith*, ed. Karl Lehmann and Albert Raffelt (New York: Crossroad Publishing, 1986) 18.

[8] John O'Donnell, *The Mystery of the Triune God* (New York: Paulist Press, 1990) 146–50.

The Spirit makes Christ contemporary with each epoch, enables prayer and explores and reveals God to each age.[9]

There is a profoundly personal element to spirituality. Its origin is in the countless ways humans encounter God in everyday life. These encounters have been known to alter an individual's existence or deeply confirm a previously chosen path. Without doubt these encounters with God lie at the center of all prayer.

The experience of God draws a person more deeply into contact with reality: the reality of God, self and others. If one truly encounters God then that person will learn what concerns God, and what certainly, but not exclusively, concerns God is the human condition.

For the Christian tradition, in the context of the Trinitarian God, it is the incarnation that founds any experiential base for spirituality. The incarnation, the unity of the divine with the human, is the Christian symbol which guides the direction of any effort to connect prayer and conscience. An incarnational spirituality enables one to look directly at the human condition rather than "averting our gaze" exclusively to some celestial vision.[10]

Relative to our present work we can look upon spirituality as the mutually corrective relationship between prayer and moral life.[11] This relationship is based upon a reappropriation of past experiences of encountering God and a corresponding intellectual critique of this experience. These encounters with God are the key basis for Christian spirituality and found prayer within reality. Christian prayer implies a thrust away from the escapism of self-centered existence and a movement toward intimacy with God.

> [Christian prayer is] a personal, intimate and profound dialogue between man and God. It expresses, therefore, the communion of redeemed creatures with the intimate life of the persons of the Trinity. This communion . . . implies an attitude of conversion, a flight from "self" to the "you" of God. [T]he essential element of authentic Christian prayer is the meeting of two freedoms, the infinite freedom of God with the finite freedom of man.[12]

In this meeting of two freedoms is the dynamic of obedience, the virtue we looked at in the previous chapter. Obedience to God is the unifying

[9] O'Donnell, *Mystery of the Triune God*, 149

[10] Kenneth Leech, *Experiencing God: Theology as Spirituality* (San Francisco: Harper and Row, 1989) 347–49.

[11] Geoffrey Wainwright, *Doxology* (New York: Oxford University Press, 1980) 410, 424.

[12] Catholic Church, Congregation for the Doctrine of the Faith, "Some Aspects of Christian Meditation," *Origins* 19:30 (December 28, 1989) 493.

element between moral sensibilities and worship or prayer. Only in rapt listening to God can persons really say they have surrendered to the divine and thus lived the life of faith and morals. To pray effectively one must be open to God and to God's transforming action. Fruitless worship is always a sign of the presence of either sin or ignorance.[13] In fact, worship and prayer are necessary so that one may have his or her moral vision clarified and renewed. Since sacred and secular are necessarily distinguished until the eschaton, their enduring tension becomes our hope in bringing us to worship and anticipating that someday God will be all in all (1 Corinthians 15). The sacred and secular, the divine and human, will remain in a tension until the end. In prayer, any dichotomy between secular and sacred is corrected by the recognition that the moral life can expand into prayer (affirming faith) and that prayer opens one up to the moral life (affirming the secular).[14]

Aspects of Prayer

Prayer should be at the symbolic center of any believer's ethic since it orients one to live out his or her dignity as beloved of God. Prayer activates the memory of being loved by God, which can deepen the reverence that one holds for him or herself and others. Out of this reverence for God, self, and others, a person is better prepared to decide what the correct moral behavior is in any situation. Moreover, this center, prayer, cannot be reduced to a sentimental appendage awkwardly clinging to one's "more important" act of moral deliberation. For the Christian it is out of prayer that any moral judgment and activity will flow.[15] Prayer is a constitutive facet of Christian ethical deliberation because prayer is a constitutive fact of being Christian. Further, the act of praying, in itself, is a profound act of morality as by it one gives to God what is God's due: a listening human heart.

According to Catholic tradition, the most direct and intimate meeting of morality and prayer occurs in the operations of conscience. "According to Scripture it is the heart that prays. . . . The heart is our hidden center . . . the place of decision . . . the place of truth, the place of encounter."[16] A person's conscience is immersed in a whole formation process and is not suspended above contexts and communities. In this process a person is embedded within the signs, symbols, rites and

---

[13] Wainwright, *Doxology,* 403.
[14] Wainwright, *Doxology,* 409–10.
[15] John Paul II, *Veritatis Splendor,* 64.
[16] CCC 2562–2563.

doctrine of a community and by this a moral character is being etched through a communal "reciprocity of consciences."[17]

Prayer takes its place within the matrix of a faith-ethic dialogue fully cognizant of its power (the stance of one who seeks God's will out of love) and its perennial temptation (circumventing human processes of responsible thinking) in favor of oracles. "The Fall" did not obliterate the continuous self-offering of God to his people as God is creating them, but sin did damage our knowledge and will to act upon the Good. Prayer, therefore, focuses the believer explicitly upon the fruit of redemption, the core of living, the divine-human exchange.

Christian prayer strives for an encounter with God as other, an encounter which begins and is sustained in humility. It is an encounter which is receptive to God and ready to yield over the self. All of this, however, is not accomplished on some level of mystification but in and through one's concrete daily commitments, relationships and achievements. In prayer one is known as beloved sinner and from this identity, and out of the strength it incurs, the person moves out, is converted, and is sustained in this conversion through the cultivation of virtue.

In prayer we are assisted by the Holy Spirit to see things as they really are. We come to realize our dependency upon God and this frees us to do the morally right thing in love. Over time, in prayer, any illusions about an autonomous self are winnowed away and one's authentic self as constitutively related to God is clarified. Ultimately, the pray-er who converses with God within the context of Christian symbols and worship has a better chance of avoiding delusion. Prayer works against the collapse of the true self into an idiocy or an individualism yielding skewed answers to ethical questions. Prayer accomplishes this not as its primary object but as the fruit of divine adoration and love.[18]

Prayer in the context of moral decision-making appears then to be an act of fidelity to one's deepest intelligent freedom before God in Christ.[19] This description of prayer encompasses the fundamental

[17] Bernard Häring, *Free and Faithful in Christ*, vol. 1 (New York: Seabury Press/ Crossroad Publishing, 1978) 265. See also James Hanigan, *Homosexuality: A Test Case for Christian Ethics* (New York: Paulist Press, 1988) 160–66.

[18] Denis Edwards, *Human Experience and God* (New York: Paulist Press, 1983) 110–11. "Decisions should be made when a person has found a certain amount of freedom. This freedom is called indifference in the Ignatian discernment tradition, and is given by Christ in prayer. A real attachment to Jesus creates the possibility of going beyond attachment to one direction and toward a real openness to accept God's will."

[19] See Karl Rahner, *Christian at the Crossroads* (New York: Seabury Press, 1975) 67–68.

identity of the human (intelligent freedom) being explicitly offered to God in Christ. A prayer-imbued ethic simply recognizes the reasonableness of discerning ethical action out of one's love for God. And so, prayer integrates intellect, will, and affection in one burst of love toward God and in that act of prayer one's identity as thinker and lover is known and received anew. Prayer is thinking with God out of love for God in Christ. Prayer is an engagement of "presences." It is an encounter with the Divine person at the level of self-exchange through a union of free intelligent beings. This engagement of presences leads to a deeper awareness of those things that concern God. It is, in other words, an awakening to a moral sense. The aim of being present to God, of being open, is the cultivation of a conscience which acknowledges not only ethical principles but the prayerful "free and unrestricted" rule of the Holy Spirit.[20]

The prayer-imbued person is cognizant of his or her own unique identity, and yet retains this within an ecclesial and cultural conversation. The attitude of prayerfulness in the Christian propels him or her to acknowledge the need to stir up love for the moral good, not simply consent to a well-developed argument.[21] At the source of Christian ethics is prayer's powerful role of orienting the human heart to its identity as God's beloved and as servant to others' needs. Persons could not be free to be faithfully Christian if God's presence was denied them, if prayer and worship were thwarted. In fact, the formation of Christian moral character is contingent upon openness to the presence of God. "We believe that the totality of existence is a longing for final fulfillment, and we believe that *through the presence of God . . .* we can distinguish the longings of the heart for goodness, from the cravings of selfishness."[22]

Placing the moral life and the life of prayer in the context of the presence of God is superior to moral virtue alone because of prayer's vigor in directing all else to God's glory. When one loves God and is devoted to God the affection of prayer can be trusted. Further, when these affections are contextualized within the Church there is less chance of one's conscience descending into *idiocy*, a habit of isolated decision-making. And, alternately in order for church leadership not to descend into *tyranny* they also must be rooted in prayer. Being in the presence of God orients the affections to a worthy object and therefore is integral to the discernment process.

[20] Hans Urs von Balthasar, *Who is A Christian?*, trans. John Cumming (Westminster, Md.: Newman Press, 1967) 86.

[21] G. Simon Harak, *Virtuous Passions: The Formation of Christian Character* (New York: Paulist Press, 1993).

[22] Bernard Häring, *Ethics of Manipulation* (New York: Seabury Press, 1975) 76.

In the end, prayer brings a knowledge which comes from love. As Roberta Bondi notes, "Only the presence of real love could be the basis of seeing the truth at all. Love and rationality must be all of a piece. Reasoning . . . is only reliable when it is grounded in love."[23] John Dunne explains that prayerful attention to God's presence yields no magical answers to ethical dilemmas, but the virtues needed to endure the commitment to love and reason to the moral truth.

> It is through the sense of presence that I come to know whatever I know of the thought of God's heart. . . . When I am at a cross-roads . . . and I ask God to show me the way, the response I seem to get from God in prayer is simply "I am with you." . . . The presence of God does help, does support me, and although it does not take away the agony of decision, it gives me the courage, the freedom to make a choice. So it is one thing simply to choose and another to choose in the Presence.[24]

A Spirit-Filled Conscience

As we noted in chapter three, prudence, that practical moral virtue that helps us to find and implement appropriate means to achieve rational ends, is significant for conscience and faith development. Leaning upon ancient philosophical thought, Simon Harak summarizes conscience and prudence quite clearly when he says, "It is not only in the province of virtue that we act the right way. It is in the province of virtue . . . that we are moved in the right way, at the right time, to the right extent. That we are first of all, moved by a passion to God."[25] Further he states that agency is not simply about transitive agency but an imminent agency which carries motive and intention, "that of being an agent for, acting on behalf of, an other . . . we are all supposed to be agents of God."[26] To be an agent for God can be most aptly expressed through one's obedience to conscience. This obedience is a positive and liberating form of listening as we noted in the previous chapter. "The obedience of judgment results . . . from the concurrence of the will and of reason, inasmuch as the loving will (called 'devota' by St. Ignatius) prompts reason, through love, to appropriate as its own the ways of

[23] Roberta Bondi, *To Pray and To Love: Conversations on Prayer with the Early Church* (Minneapolis, Minn.: Fortress Press, 1991) 36.

[24] John Dunne, *Love's Mind: An Essay on the Contemplative Life* (Notre Dame, Ind.: University of Notre Dame Press, 1993) 41.

[25] Harak, *Virtuous Passions*, 96.

[26] Harak, *Virtuous Passions*, 96–97.

seeing belonging to another."[27] In listening to conscience, the person cleaves to the good, the true, and hence to God, thus becoming God's agent. The one who can approach ethical deliberation with this "devota" is truly humble and thus available to the truth as recognized by reason.

In the prayerful conscience, the believer appropriates the moral truth out of love for it and for God. As John Paul II has taught, "It is the heart converted to the Lord and to the love of what is good which is really the source of true judgments of conscience. . . . Knowledge of God's law in general is certainly necessary but not sufficient: what is essential is a sort of connaturality between man and the true good."[28] It is the Spirit working within us which frees us to obey, not out of compulsion, but out of love. The Holy Spirit, who loves us from within and to whom we look in love, frees us to listen by appeal not coercion. The seeking of God out of love and the seeking of moral truth are at once the Holy Spirit operating as conscience.[29] By adhering to the Holy Spirit within, we simultaneously stand with God and in this world, open to divine wisdom and utilizing human reasoning. Apart from this openness to the Spirit dwelling within us everything "goes wrong epistemologically. Prayer becomes a frustrated soliloquy and knowledge of God is redacted to a form of objectified self-understanding."[30] The Spirit dwelling within can be understood essentially as the Sprit of truth active within us when we listen for God's will.[31]

God's Voice

We are aware of the need to discern whether the moral obligation detected by conscience is true or not. In other words, is this "voice"[32] simply superego or social convention and not God's wisdom penetrating the intellect? Of course parental command or societal convention can convey God's wisdom, but it must be discerned as such. Discerning the

---

[27] Peter Henrici, "The Spiritual Dimension and Its Form of Reason," *Communio* 20 (Winter 1993) 646.

[28] John Paul II, *Veritatis Splendor*, 64.

[29] Karl Rahner, *The Spirit in the Church* (New York: Seabury Press, 1979) 30–31. See also James Hanigan, "Conscience and the Holy Spirit," *CTSA Proceedings of the Fifty-first Annual Convention*, 227–46.

[30] T. F. Torrance, *God and Rationality* (London: Oxford University Press, 1971) 205.

[31] Yves Congar, *I Believe in the Holy Spirit*, trans. David Smith (New York: Seabury Press, 1983) 102.

[32] See *Gaudium et Spes* 16. In this paragraph, the Council Fathers refer to the judgment of conscience as the place where the "voice of God" resounds.

voice of God within the command of conscience implies that a whole pastoral formation regimen is being or has been experienced. As noted in the previous chapter one must be formed in virtue in the context of worship, word and service to the poor to recognize more clearly the promptings of God from within. And of course even with this formation sin is still pervasive and one can go astray. However, for the Christian a faith-filled conscience formation is the *only* way to limit the self-deception incurred by sin's insidious and sometimes all too subtle presence within persons. The judgment of conscience itself is not infallibly revelatory of the divine mind. When the Christian is actually convinced, however, of the final judgment of conscience, this judgment is to be considered practically ultimate as a response to God and thus is a form of prayer. Loving God and obeying one's conscience out of love is not only the clearest sign of Christian freedom, but in its depth encompasses the essential dynamics of prayer.

So the judgment of conscience can be an explicit encounter with God for the believer. It is a very sacred moment as testified to in the Catholic doctrine that the judgment of conscience must never be disobeyed. In this judgment one receives the strength and wisdom to do the right thing but only as the culmination of one's open engagement with solid formational sources. Since faith tells a person that God only wills one's good it is reasonable to assume that in the process of making one's judgment God is communicating with that person through the very goodness of human intellectual and volitional powers. We are free so that God might address us from within our hearts. This experience of the judgment of conscience as carrying divine communication is not a full blown private mystical revelation but simply an experience of thinking out of love, a love that fastens onto God as its object. In other words, the voice of God is not the face of God. Nevertheless, As David Platt has noted, "If morality is simply a product of social conditioning how is it that time and again in history, individuals have brought society into question and have judged society morally deficient? Religious empiricists have paid too much attention to dramatic mystical encounters and not enough to the still small voice which may ever so gently impinge on consciousness."[33]

Understanding the judgment of conscience as prayer-imbued makes explicit the tenet that reason can see more clearly when devoted to Christ rather than clouded over by self-centeredness. Prayer, as an expression of faith, suffuses all reasonable searching for and judgment of the moral good. The judgment of conscience as suffused in prayer

---

[33] David Platt, "Divinity as Given," *International Philosophical Quarterly* 27 (December 1987) 391–92.

simply renders explicit the presence of the love of God where some may be tempted to reduce the context to reason alone. In accepting obedience to conscience as an act of prayer one accepts the operations of conscience as fallible and yet open to the true and good's ultimate foundation in God. With this understanding, both deciding what is right and becoming a good person meet in the believer's thinking with God out of love for God in Christ and in the conscience judgments that flow from that thinking.

It is the person's availability and openness to be taught by the judgment of conscience that constitutes the prayerfulness in any of its imperatives. It is not the presence of an infallible moral judgment that indicates one has listened to the voice of God. The docility to the moral action, either rightly or wrongly perceived in the conscience imperative, is an act of listening to the voice of God. The imperative of conscience is God's voice to that person, in those specific circumstances, at that time. If obeyed, the person wills to do what he or she judges to be ethical and therefore wills to obey God.

Edward Vacek has argued that there is danger in emphasizing conscience as the voice of God at the level of actual judgment. It may, he says, lead one simply to reduce Christian ethics to obedience to authority.

> For Pope John Paul II, conscience is the voice of God. There are dangers in such a position. Persons or institutions . . . may claim that what they think is unqualifiedly what God is thinking. [In response, some may say that the phrase "voice of God"] means that conscience is dependent on the objective moral order and on God. [Yet,] . . . insisting on submission to the moral norm [objective moral order] does not provide any place for the proper role of our reason in discovering and creating the moral good. If we are to cooperate, we must do so in a fully human way; that means our reason must have something of its own to contribute, in however dependent a way. Our personhood is not fully engaged if all we are supposed to do is to discover some pre-existent law and then conform.[34]

Though moral norms are indeed binding, conformity to them is not a sign that one is less than "fully engaged" as a person. Even in obedience to pre-established norms, the act of conformity should, in fact, be an act of the person seized by the truth of that norm. In this way even conformity is a personal act. Vacek himself alludes to this quality when

---

[34] Edward Vacek, "John Paul II and Cooperation with God," *The Annual of the Society of Christian Ethics*, ed. D. M. Yeager (Knoxville, Tenn.: University of Tennessee, 1990) 98–99.

he notes that "reason must have something of its own to contribute, in however dependent a way." This dependency is primarily at the foundational level of conscience, the level where God sustains us and communicates his "voice" through a general call to goodness, a call that stirs our desire to do and be good. Dependency is also expressed, however, at the level of practical judgment in the obedience to truth that the person adheres to whether or not the conscience knows such truth through a moral norm or some "creative" contribution. We would agree with Josef Fuchs when he says:

> A moral system . . . must call itself innovative, if what it says does not exclusively mean the adoption of something that already exists. It must have its own innovative element; something that is not already contained in what exists but derives from the person making the ethical decision even if it is only the judgment that an ethical answer that already exists is the correct answer, *in concreto*, to the person's problem.[35]

Note that in appropriating an already existing moral norm *as one's own* a person is fully engaged as a moral agent.

In coming to moral judgments, what would characterize Christian ethics if it was built upon a sense of the personal and interpersonal? Faith sheds light on ethics in distinctive fashion. But if faith is further delineated in piety, worship and prayer, will one's approach to moral decision-making be unique beyond simple acknowledgement of faith? What would life be like if one turned from worldly wisdom, from the security of obeying law, and trusted in the Spirit of God to lead and validate the self? What would life be like if one listened to the Divine Spirit in freedom and relinquished the gods created due to fear? What in other words would life be like if one loved God?

For the discerning person who loves God in Jesus Christ, it will be precisely this love which organizes and unifies his or her life into a constant whole. It is not simply a reasonable dictate regarding the truth which conscience communicates, not simply the norms, but an echo, a word, grounded in a divine address rather than self-sufficiency.[36] This divine address in the context of a reasonable dictate is not made as a strikingly disparate tension, however. As Karl Rahner argued, even the nonbeliever who responds to appeals of love from neighbor is responding to an implied divine address (see Matthew 25). For the Church,

[35] Josef Fuchs, *Moral Demands and Personal Obligations* (Washington, D.C.: Georgetown, 1993) 114.

[36] Alistair I. McFadyen, *The Call to Personhood: A Christian Theory of the Individual in Social Relationships* (New York: Cambridge, 1990).

however, it is important to retain the theologically explicit conceptual language of such an appeal because of the public evangelical mission of Catholicism.[37] The church does not simply articulate a philosophy but *faith* seeking understanding.

Focusing upon the indwelling voice of the Spirit assists the believer in retaining a personal engagement with God. Mark O'Keefe has said:

> Christians must make their decisions in light of the promptings of the Holy Spirit whose voice speaks from within. [The virtues, gifts of the Holy Spirit and infused virtues]—especially as perfected by the operation of charity and the gifts of counsel and wisdom—demonstrates (Thomas') belief in the importance of non-rational and Spirit-guided elements of Christian choosing . . . Christians . . . must grow in prayer and in their relationship with God, so that they can become accustomed to recognizing and responding to the voice of the Spirit.[38]

Situating prayer in the context of conscience judgment is an explicit way of affirming that God accepts us in our struggles to discern good from evil, that this process is soaked in divine support. God is not impartially awaiting our discernment on the sidelines. God loves us. We cannot control God in our prayerful discernment; rather "we yield to God the power to personally influence us."[39]

Seeing conscience in a matrix of prayer positively contextualizes a role for, and an understanding of, the nature of loving obedience to God. It is not legalistic or authoritarian to obey the imperative of conscience as God's voice. It is an act of autonomy to become obedient and hence human dignity is preserved, not undermined, in obeying the divine voice in the imperative of conscience.

It is reasonable to obey the divine voice unconditionally in the conscience imperative when such a God is known to will the well-being of humans as embodied in Jesus through mercy, justice, and wisdom. Through the presence of the indwelling Spirit these attributes, and others, resound in us as worthy of divine and human dignity and "make unconditional obedience to His will a reasonable solution to the problem of morality."[40] For the person of faith to decide morally relevant

---

[37] Jean Porter, "Salvific Love and Charity," *The Love Commandments: Essays in Christian Ethics and Moral Philosophy* (Washington, D.C.: Georgetown, 1992) 257.

[38] Mark O'Keefe, "Discernment and Christian Moral Decision Making," *Journal of Spiritual Formation* 15 (February 1994) 79.

[39] O'Keefe, "Discernment," 79.

[40] Chan Coulter, "Moral Autonomy and Divine Commands," *Religious Studies* 25 (1989) 129.

questions in isolation from God appears counterintuitive. This process of listening to conscience in all its components is tantamount to what Rahner called the prayer of decision. This prayer involves decisions which reach down to a person's very foundation.

> On such decision depends the very foundation of our relationship with God . . . hence the great significance for time and eternity of these moments of decision. They become moments of lived prayer, when a man chooses to make God's decision. They cannot be other than the very essence of prayer, since they are practical answers to the sweet insistence of Divine love. Hence when we speak of the prayer of decision, we mean that lived prayer in every decision made in accordance with the will of God.[41]

Making decisions in accord with the voice of God promotes a further way to embrace personalism and reject legalism. But at the same time, it contextualizes a more positive role for, and understanding of, the nature of obedience to God. This approach, in the end, is more akin to Rahner's sense of dialogue ("they become moments of lived prayer, when a man chooses to make God's decision").

The inner connection between prayer and moral living *is* the distinct element in Christian ethics.[42] The presence of God is a crucial factor in discerning right and wrong. Discipleship releases us to live out of our conscience and therefore to be free. In this freedom the disciple is morally certain that in a genuine search for, and discovery of moral truth, conscience is to be trusted as the practical voice of God.

A Faith-filled Reason

Since prayer is a function of an affectively imbued reason (thinking *with* God out of love *for* God in Jesus Christ), it grasps the objective reality which right and wrong is based upon not as oracle but upon the same ground *as* reason and *by* reason. However, by making prayer explicit one emphasizes the fact that the reason of believers is imbued with faith. In the believer reason's basis and ground is acknowledged to be in God. This more fully articulates a believer's anthropology and epistemology. Of course, Christians can reason to moral decisions without explicit reference to God, but why do it? To do so would be like a married person saying that he or she can reason to decisions about

---

[41] Karl Rahner, *Prayer* (New York: Paulist Press, 1968) 99.
[42] Enda McDonagh, *Doing the Truth: The Quest for Moral Theology* (Notre Dame, Ind.: University of Notre Dame Press, 1979) 60.

married life without reference to his or her spouse and to how that relationship totally molds their world. Of course the spouse *can* reason
without this reference but it is reasoning separated from the fullness of
that person's reality. Deleting references to God cannot make Christian
ethical deliberation any more authentic or objective, but it can make it
unfaithful. David Schindler has made similar conclusions regarding
morality in his criticism of the American culture of liberalism. "American Liberalism does not deny God explicitly but it fails to integrate the
creature's constitutive relation to God into the workings of culture."[43]

Analogously, to remove the voice of God from the judgment of conscience is to fail to integrate one's constitutive relation to God into the
workings of moral deliberation. Removing the "voice" metaphor facili-
tates a practical atheism in Christian ethics, resulting in a moral judgment which does not allow or is passively indifferent to the affect, or
influence, of the presence of God. But how does one know whether
conscience is truly the "voice of God" or, as we explored in chapter one,
it is simply being called that due to the impact of "a mystical culture"?
Of course on this we only have moral certitude. It has been the long-
standing tradition of Catholic moral theology to see in the judgments
of reason attaining to truth a simultaneous participation in the "eternal
law of God." Catholicism argues, in other words, that reason's judgment of truth is a divine mediation. If this is not so, Catholicism could
never teach, as it does in the Second Vatican Council, that rapt listening
to the judgment of conscience is salvific.[44]

This emphasis on prayer does not require calling God "on stage," as
it were, simply during a time of ethical decision. The divine presence is
perceived and engaged as this presence organically emerges from
within one's life. There is a theological consensus in the Catholic
Church that those who do not explicitly acknowledge God as their conversation partner in a search for moral truth can still achieve that truth.
However, for the believer to act like a nonbeliever in the act of searching for, and judging, moral truth is to undermine his or her fidelity to
discipleship.

Living in Reality

Understanding the conscience as prayerful reflects the fullness of
one's reality as a communal or ecclesial person who has been chosen
by, and made responsive to God in Christ. To judge right from wrong

---

[43] David Schindler, "The Culture of Love," *The Catholic World Report* (October
1994) 46.

[44] *Lumen Gentium* 16; CCC 847.

out of this perspective contextualizes in reality more fully the discernment process and moral judgment one eventually attains.

Prayer opens one to the fullness of his or her identity in Christ, and thus that agent decides out of the strength of that identity. One's identity in Christ, as sustained by the indwelling of the Trinity, establishes the very teaching of the Church that one ought never to disobey conscience.[45] In fact, the only reason *fundamental conscience,* understood as the call from God to simply be and choose the good, and, in our position, *situational conscience* as well, understood as one's judgment about a concrete decision, can be said to have an absolute claim over us is due to its capacity to listen to the divine voice. Josef Fuchs reserves the appelation "voice of God" only to fundamental conscience and not to specific judgments of conscience. This is because only fundamental conscience is infallible in its orienting the person to the good. This infallibility is experienced in the person's apprehension of moral first principles (do good and avoid evil), in the person's sense of being a moral creature, and in the challenge and readiness to act rightly. This is the experience of the "voice of God" in conscience, and it arises from the person's being constituted within God's creation, not by any "special categorical intervention" from God.[46] This fundamental operation of conscience, as it grasps "the good," may be called the voice of God because it can "be derived directly from God through the creation of the human person who is God's image."[47] Thus, for Fuchs, the only infallible voice of God in conscience resides in the fundamental conscience as the command to seek the good and be ready to follow it. The person seeking the good, and open to the objective ethical order in the fundamental conscience, is adhering to the voice of God.[48] Also, Fuchs specifies what he calls situational conscience. Situational conscience operates in the act of judging a concrete behavior as right or wrong. Situational conscience is open to error, and hence cannot be understood as the voice of God "in the same sense" as fundamental conscience.[49] We presume that he means in the sense that fundamental conscience judgment is "infallible," and situational is not.

Norbert Rigali comments:

---

[45] CCC 1790.

[46] Josef Fuchs, "The Absolute in Morality and the Christian Conscience," *Gregorianum* 71 (1990) 706. See also Fuchs, "Conscience and Conscientious Fidelity," ed. Charles Curran, *Moral Theology: Challenges for the Future* (New York: Paulist Press, 1990) 112.

[47] Fuchs, "Conscience and Conscientious Fidelity," 112.

[48] Fuchs, "The Absolute in Morality," 707.

[49] Fuchs, "Conscience and Conscientious Fidelity," 113.

> Every person knows that an individual may never act contrary to
> his own honest conscience. . . . This notion, however, would be
> the pinnacle of pride if conscience were nothing more than a
> person's taking counsel with himself or his own freedom. If God
> were not present in conscience, an individual's following his own
> conscience in the face of universal disagreement with him would
> be the peak of egoism, an act of setting oneself above the rest of
> mankind.[50]

Rigali is not simply thinking of the presence of God in the first principles of fundamental conscience but is referring to an actual judgment
of conscience in the concrete. This is similar to Rahner's formal existential ethic, wherein he argues for a "divinely inspired individual impulse" to be recognized in and by the Church.[51]

Could not an existential ethics help us to see more clearly that sin,
over and above its property of being an offence against the law of God,
is also and just as much an offence against an utterly individual imperative of the individual will of God, which is the basis of uniqueness?
Would we not perceive sin more clearly in this way as the failure of the
personal-individual love of God?[52]

Rahner does not argue that this Divine imperative is uttered in con-
tradiction to any established norm but simply highlights that ethics is
personal and is not exhausted by simply applying norms deductively
to ethical questions in concrete situations.[53] Newman also made space
for the well-formed conscience to follow the truth wherever it leads
even in opposition to the "supreme, though not infallible Authority of
the Pope."[54] Newman's qualification for opposing papal teaching is
germane. He says, "Unless a man is able to say to himself, as in the
Presence of God, that he must not, and dare not, act upon the Papal injunction, he is bound to obey it."[55]

The term, "as in the presence of God," implies a personal judgment
of conscience by one who has been ushered into the divine presence by
way of the operations of conscience. Note also how stringent Newman's standard for dissent was in this particular writing; if I obey the

---

[50] Norbert Rigali, "Morality as an Encounter with God," *Cross and Crown* 26 (Sep-
tember 1974) 266.

[51] Rahner, *Theological Investigations*, trans. Karl-H. Kruger, vol. 2 (New York: Crossroad Publishing, 1990) 233.

[52] Rahner, *Theological Investigations*, 2:232.

[53] Rahner, *Theological Investigations*, 2:222.

[54] Newman, *Certain Difficulties Felt by Anglicans in Catholic Teaching Considered*,
vol. 2 (New York: Longmans, Green, & Co., 1900–01) 257.

[55] Newman, *Certain Difficulties*, 258.

Pope on this matter I will be sinning, therefore I cannot obey the Pope. What both Rahner and Newman seem to hold here is that God can communicate to an individual through the situational conscience. And, even though it might be rare, God can summon one to obey individually the conscience beyond the norm[56] and even in opposition to non-infallible teaching. In allowing for this divine communication through the conscience, both Newman and Rahner highlight the dignity of the individual by reason of the indwelling Spirit gifted to the whole Church.[57] Hans Rotter summarizes this stance well:

> How does one find the power to act ethically . . . from oughts, human fellowship and goodwill, or from Jesus Christ and His Spirit (Gal. 5:1)? . . . Ethical strength—beyond fulfilling norm—is found to the extent that that person relates to life with inspiration and enthusiasm. . . . The encounter with Jesus Christ in prayer gives man a new possibility for freedom. . . . The endangering of Christian ethics in our time is not due to lack of empirical knowledge or rational penetration but to the fact that Christian *faith* and *spirituality* are endangered.[58]

Both Rahner and Newman recognize in persons the freedom to listen to conscience because they have been convinced that the "encounter with Jesus Christ in prayer gives man a new possibility of freedom." And this encounter occurs par excellence in the docility of a person toward his or her conscience and its imperatives.

Here is how both fundamental and situational conscience, understood as prayerful, better assists the individual to grasp the objective reality of deciding right and wrong; it grounds the agent in the freedom needed to know and respond to the truth which the believer loves in Jesus. In prayer one is freed from illusory loves and disordered affections and directed to God as one's principal love.

Perhaps one has developed the habit of prayer and thus has had his or her character fashioned by this intimacy; this does not, however, give the pray-er any better access to infallible ethical reasoning than the non-pray-er. The truth of this principle notwithstanding, it generally appears to facilitate one to veer toward what Michael Mendiola calls

---

[56] For instance, think of those "dissenters" during World War II who tried to claim Conscientious Objector status as Catholics when the then applicable church teaching saw that claim as impossible for the lay Catholic male to hold during a just war. See Germain Grisez, *Living a Christian Life*, The Way of the Lord Jesus Ser. 2 (Quincy, IL: Franciscan Press, 1993) 206–7.

[57] Rahner, *Theological Investigations*, 2:230.

[58] Hans Rotter, "Spirituality and Moral Renewal," *Theology Digest* 27 (1979) 13–14.

impartial rationality.[59] In this position one seems to artificially separate the context and narrative of a person's life from his or her intellectual deliberations.

> The canon of impartial rationality fictitiously abstracts the moral agent from . . . religious experience. If not impartial rationality then what kind of rationality. . . . ? [Faith] is thus correlative to practical, as distinct from pure, speculative reason, that is, the reason of a self, rather than of impersonal mind, which must struggle with those problems and obscurities in life that trouble us not as "observers of life" but as "moral agents and sufferers."[60]

Situating Christian ethics in the context of the believer's commitment to love God in Jesus and to think out of the substance of this commitment in ethical deliberation realistically reconnects the agent to his or her authentic ground of decision-making. This ground is not the self, the ecclesial authority, or the current stream of philosophy's latest word, but rather the perennial appeal of God through the personally embraced communal faith of Christianity as reasonably reflected upon. This appeal is heard most authoritatively in the conscience. And it is a voice which directs its listener not to a more and more isolated path of decision-making but one open to the Spirit in community. In this listening one prays.

Christian Spirituality and the Prayer-Imbued Conscience

Since the judgment of conscience is fundamentally prayerful then prayer stands as essential and intrinsic to all ethical decisions that spring from one's interiority. But this is different from holding that "saying prayers" directly "enlightens the criterion for what makes a decision right or wrong." Of course, prayers alone will not give appropriate criteria for ethical decisions, unless one has a private revelation.[61] However, a contextualized understanding of the judgment of conscience as fundamentally prayerful resists any solipsistic undermining of authentic moral judgment. One's love of God and deliberation about

[59] See Michael Mendiola, "Bioethics and Impartial Rationality: The Search for Neutrality," *Religious Methods and Resources in Bioethics*, ed. Paul Camenisch (Dordrecht: Kluwer, 1994) 154–58.

[60] Mendiola, "Bioethics and Impartial Rationality," 157, 158.

[61] See Kenneth Himes, O.F.M., "Prayer and the Moral Life: Tracing the Connection," *Listening* 34:3 (Fall 1999) 180–91.

what is right behavior in the matrix of Catholic commitment and tradition holds a broader and deeper assurance that we have "done our best" in ethical thinking and moral judgment.

The loss of freedom for the person, both before and during dialogue with God, is one temptation in current moral theory and method (positivistic tendencies). The loss of God's freedom to appeal to the agent is a second temptation (rationalistic tendencies). Seeing conscience in a prayerful matrix elicits assistance from Christian spirituality in moral theology's perennial struggle against these two temptations.

When the judgment of conscience is understood to involve prayer, Christian ethics is placed in a better position to engage Christian spirituality. Formation in ethics must not be based simply on principles, methods and law but on humanity's openness to the Divine. Christian ethics is grounded in *orthodoxia*, a church formed in the adoration and worship of God. Since prayer is a thinking out of love, love of God takes on a significant formational role, and a place for explicit piety and devotion is recognized in Christian ethics.

The prayer-imbued conscience is a paradox of acquisition and gift, of knowledge and love, neither of which cancels the other, but rather, taken as a whole facilitate the habit of seeking the truth. "The heart [or conscience] becomes . . . a symbol for acting from the core of one's being and with a consciousness constituted by a higher operational synthesis of all three strands of consciousness: affection, cognition, and volition."[62]

Christian spirituality is the concrete living out of one's love for Jesus. It defies theorizing and cries out for authentic living anchored in God's eternal union with all that is human through the coming of Christ. The core of the prayer-imbued conscience is Christian spirituality's foundational experience: humans are addressed by God in Christ through the Church, and this address is what founds and orients one toward reality. Authentic Christian spirituality is definite and palpable.

> It is clear that if we claim to have a concept of, say, charity, at all, then we must be able to say what charity looks like—what the charitable person characteristically does. . . . Greed is associated with specific kinds of situations and particular appetites, whereas charity, as an architectonic virtue, is not so particularized. Nonetheless, Aquinas indicates sufficiently how we are to recognize charity as an enduring trait of character, by spelling out the kinds of dispositions and enduring orientations that it produces. . . . Specifically, what we observe, over the course of a lifetime, is the

---

[62] Andrew Tallon, "Affection, Cognition, Volition: The Triadic Meaning of Heart in Ethics," *American Catholic Philosophical Quarterly* 68:2 (1994) 229.

way in which various actions and character traits of an individual are brought into a unity by a conscious orientation toward the God of Jesus Christ. And that unity looks different from the life of the upright pagan, or indeed, that of the unloving Christian.[63]

Hence, in drawing attention to the prayerful quality of the conscience imperative both the explicit moral judgment found in that act and the implied openness to receive and participate in the Mystery which is God are unified. For the believer both her love for God and her love for neighbor can be explicitly acknowledged in the judgment of conscience, and therefore her faithful activity can be drawn from the fullness of her life, the entire reality of her commitments. This understanding of moral judgment expresses a fuller sense of Christian spiritual living.

Prayer is an opening to reality just as reason is, but in thinking about God, out of love for Christ, there is a distinctive nuance. The language of Lorenzo Albacete is expressive of this nuance in the prayer-imbued conscience; it is an activity of "thinking-with that occurs when being-with."[64] What should interest the Christian is not "subjectivity" but rather "interiority" and the communion with God in Christ which interiority implies. The Christian does not simply seek the "innards of the human self" but the very presence of God. "Prayer . . . is the means by which we go within ourselves in order to stand before God on that broad 'fair field.'"[65] The interior communion between the person and his or her God expressed in the prayer-imbued conscience is a partial glimpse into the very heart of reality itself.

> It is the lack of depth that is so striking, so wearying, so desolate in much of the talk about subjectivity and the interiority of the self today. For the distinctive sense of Christian concreteness is found in the irreplaceable worth of each finite thing,—its dignity, its worthiness, not simply as a finite being, but precisely as creature. The creature's dignity stems from the presence of God intimately bound with the creature; and that intimacy is the very dignity-conferring love of God for each creature. No amount of talk about autonomy, freedom, coming of age and independence can confer that absolute dignity upon human beings and the world.[66]

[63] Porter, "Salvific Love and Charity," 254.

[64] Lorenzo Albacete, "The Relevance of Christ or the *sequela Christi*," *Communio* 21 (Summer 1994) 255, 257, 258.

[65] Kenneth Schmitz, "Concrete Presence," *Communio* 14 (Fall 1987) 304. See also Himes, "Prayer and The Moral Life: Tracing the Connection," 181ff.

[66] Schmitz, "Concrete Presence," 313, 314.

We wish to relate obedience to conscience with listening to God and thus with prayer, but this relation is practical. Of course obedience to conscience, per se, is not the same thing as a conscious, explicit act of saying prayers. One is definitely deciding if he or she ought to defend the common good through participation in the military, for example, and is not engaged in reciting a "Hail Mary." However, we maintain that obedience to the situational conscience is always an implied prayer, in its love for the true and the good. And for the believer it is an implication which becomes more and more explicit as faith develops. So much so that the Church can call the conscience judgment an echo of God's voice. Ultimately, the believer gives obedience, that is, lovingly listens, to a Person.

As Vacek says, "[The believer's] ethical acts are not the same as those of the atheist. Just as two people riding a train, one going to work and the other fleeing home, are not doing the same thing, even though within a limited time frame, each seems to be doing nothing more than sitting, so we and the atheist are not, on the whole, doing the same thing.[67] When the believer listens to his or her conscience this is an act of prayer; when nonbelievers respond to the truth of their conscience they are simply assenting to the moral good, and God only implicitly.

This acceptance of the prayer-imbued conscience as a key truth in the formation of conscience and the discernment of moral behavior is a vision of Christian ethics as practiced from within a Christian spirituality:

> One clue to the decline of Christian morality is the fact that the "specialists" who propound it seem to have lost all sense of its origins in and relationship to the prayer and worship of Christians. As a result, Christian ethics is often defined as a rational system of rules and principles residing in theological texts available to believer and nonbeliever alike. This way of conceiving Christian ethics . . . has become increasingly strange to (the thousands of silent believers, who worship in spirit and truth) . . . we need to rediscover the ecclesial context of Christian ethics. Christian ethics is grounded . . . not in what individual Christian ethicists write [regarding the conversation with culture via the natural law] but in what all Christians do together in community.[68]

---

[67] Edward Vacek, *Love, Human and Divine: The Heart of Christian Ethics* (Washington, D.C.: Georgetown, 1994) 140.

[68] Vigen Guroian, *Ethics after Christendom: Toward An Ecclesial Christian Ethic* (Grand Rapids: Eerdmans, 1994) 26, 40.

Chapter Five

Jesus as the Norm of the Spiritual Moral Life:
Some Pastoral Considerations

"His is authentic and absolute Truth, and without this Truth it is impossible to know the truth or to achieve salvation."[1] These words from *The Philokalia* bring to mind Jesus' words in the Gospel of John: "I am the way, and the truth, and the life; no one comes to the Father but through me" (John 14:6). Together, these sayings point to the centrality of Christ for the spiritual moral life. They underscore the relevance of Christ for every dimension of human existence and remind us that without him we can achieve very little on our own. Our knowledge of the truth is a function of our knowledge of Christ. We know Christ by being in relationship with him. We enter into and sustain a relationship with him through prayer.

In this concluding chapter we will look at some of the practical implications of what listening to Christ and his body in prayer means for conscience formation. We will do so first by examining what it means to say that Christ is the norm of the spiritual moral life and looking at its implications for the moral imagination. We will then outline the various skills involved in the "rapt listening" we are suggesting and close by treating a series of concrete cases relevant to the process of conscience formation.

---

[1] *The Philokalia: The Complete Text*, vol. 3, trans. G.E.H. Palmer, Philip Sherrard, Kallistos Ware (Boston: Faber and Faber, 1984) 321.

Christ as the Norm of the Spiritual Moral Life

The publication of Bernard Häring's *The Law of Christ* in 1954 heralded a change in Catholic moral theology by placing the person of Christ at the very heart of the discipline. From that moment on, Catholic moral theologians had to come to terms with the innovative (albeit paradoxical) insight that a concrete historical personage had universal, transhistorical significance for the understanding of human comportment. This shift in moral paradigms helped bring an end to the manualist emphasis on principles applied to case studies and applied to isolated human actions. It was also instrumental in bringing about Vatican II's call for the renewal of moral theology, which encouraged the exploration of the Biblical foundations of the Christian moral life and the obligation Christ's followers have "to bring forth fruit in charity for the life of the world."[2]

To speak of Christ as the "law" or "norm" of the Christian morality means not that Jesus' moral teachings are unique or particularly distinctive, but that he embraces in his life, death, and resurrection the epitome of that toward which all Christians (and, one might add, all human beings) ultimately tend. Norbert Rigali expresses it in this way:

> That Jesus Christ is the law of morality means that his human life is the standard by which every human life is to be measured. The task of trying to understand Jesus as the norm of the *humanum*, then, is not directly one of collecting his teachings about what people should or should not do—for example, in the Sermon on the Mount. Nor is it directly the effort of trying to discern the unity, the unified meaning, of the human life that is Jesus himself. In a word, that Jesus is the norm of the *humanum* means that his meaning, the meaning that he freely gave to his life (or, more precisely, that he freely created out of his life—this is the norm of what every *vita humana* should mean.[3]

By "the *humanum*," Rigali is referring to the whole of human life taken as the object of moral theological reflection and not isolated human acts, which the manualist tradition classically referred to *actus humanus*. By "law" or "norm," he means the "dynamically inviting possibility" that confronts human freedom and offers the human person the opportunity for self-realization. Such an understanding of Christ as the norm of the spiritual moral life extends not just to Christians but to all

---

[2] See *Optatam Totius* 16.
[3] Norbert Rigali, "Christ and Morality," in *The Distinctiveness of Christian Ethics,* eds. Charles E. Curran and Richard A. McCormick, Readings in Moral Theology No. 2 (New York/Ramsey: Paulist Press, 1980) 115.

human beings. It affirms Christ as the measure of "our natural law," for it sees in him "the law of humanity's deepest moral aspirations in history, the law of our concrete, supernaturally affected nature."[4]

A similar approach to Jesus as the norm of the spiritual moral life comes from Hans Urs von Balthasar. Known for his insistence on the intrinsic unity of Catholic theology and spirituality, Balthasar places Christ at the very center of history. "[I]n Jesus Christ," he states, "the Logos is no longer the realm of ideas, values and laws which governs and gives meaning to history but is history himself."[5] He goes on to say that "the historical life of the Logos—to which his death, resurrection and ascension belong—is, as such, that very world of ideas which, directly and indirectly or reductively, gives the norm for all history; yet not as coming forth from some non-historical height above, but from the living center of history itself."[6] Jesus, in other words, not only shares the human condition, but also has become the personal and universal norm for all human beings. He achieves this status of a universal norm by the work of the Holy Spirit, who reveals the truth of the Son, makes him personally present in the sacraments, and coordinates the life of Christ with the life of the Christian.[7]

Elsewhere, Balthasar outlines a series of theses for what it means to speak of the fulfillment of the spiritual moral life in Christ.[8] Among these, he insists that the person of Christ is the concrete, plenary, and universal norm for all moral action. In Jesus, the universal has entered concrete, historical fact. As such, we find that our destiny is intimately bound up with his: "It is for this that God created us (Eph 1:4ff.). By the power of the cross we have been given the Holy Spirit of Christ and of the Father (Rom 8:9, 11). In that Spirit the Person of Christ and his work are made present to all ages and are also at work in us. The same Spirit also makes us continually present to Christ."[9] For Balthasar, the Christian moral life is deeply integrated with life in the Spirit. In the Spirit, Christ encounters us, initiates a dialogue with us, and makes himself present as the only norm in every situation. Christian ethics, in this respect, takes on a cruciform shape, the vertical and horizontal dimensions of which can never be separated from the person of Jesus who

---

[4] Rigali, "Christ and Morality," 119.

[5] Hans Urs von Balthasar, *A Theology of History* (New York: Sheed and Ward, 1963) 18.

[6] Balthasar, *A Theology of History*, 18–19.

[7] Balthasar, *A Theology of History*, 79–107.

[8] Hans Urs von Balthasar, "Nine Theses in Christian Ethics," in *The Distinctiveness of Christian Ethics*, eds. Charles E. Curran and Richard A. McCormick, Readings in Moral Theology No. 2, (New York/Ramsey: Paulist, 1980) 190–206.

[9] Balthasar, "Nine Theses," 194.

was crucified and lifted up.[10] When seen in this light, sin becomes the refusal of divine filiation offered by God in Jesus Christ; it is the denial of Christ as a personal norm and proceeds from a spirit positively hostile to the divine and all that is truly human.[11] Conscience, by way of contrast, is "a transcendental preknowledge of revelation" which confronts us with the reality of the Absolute. It gives us an awareness of the distinction between absolute freedom and given freedom, and helps us to see the unity between the call from the Absolute and from others. Our quest for the absolute is rooted in the transcendental dialogical character of human freedom. We cannot achieve this desire for the absolute by ourselves, but need to be open to God's self-revelation in Christ to grasp the meaning of full communion with God.[12]

Presentations such as Rigali's and Balthasar's recognize Jesus as "the man for others," whose passion, death, and resurrection form the concrete salvific paradigm for all of humanity. The paradox of how an absolute norm of universal dimensions is expressed in the concrete historical personage of Jesus of Nazareth, however, is shrouded in mystery and can never be fully explained. The Christian faith affirms, however, that in the person of Jesus, the Incarnate Word made flesh, humanity has overcome death and regained in a concrete, palpable way access to the fullness of life that it lost through the sin of human origins. Hidden from history, the eternal compassion of God becomes visible in the person of Jesus and promises to reach its culmination through our growing participation through the Spirit in Christ's body, the Church. That body itself has many dimensions (models, if you will) which, together, caution us against reducing the mystery to any one of its functioning parts.[13]

This ecclesial dimension of the spiritual moral life is a primary instrument through which the Spirit enables us to get in touch with Christ. Through Christ's body, the Church, the Spirit extends the living presence of Jesus throughout time and space. As herald, servant, sacrament, mystical communion, and institution, the Church continues Jesus' mission on earth and proclaims to all cultures and to all peoples the Good News of plentiful redemption.[14] As a historical event with transhistorical consequences, the Christ event is relived in the historical sojourn of the pilgrim People of God. Drawn to the Father by the gift of the Spirit, the followers of "The Way" embody Christ's kenotic self-offering of love through the dialogic process of agapic listening

---

[10] Balthasar, "Nine Theses," 195.
[11] Balthasar, "Nine Theses," 196.
[12] Balthasar, "Nine Theses," 201–3.
[13] See Avery Dulles, *Models of the Church* (Garden City, N.Y.: Doubleday, 1974) 36.
[14] For a development of these various models, see Dulles, *Models*, esp. 39–108.

and response that sits at the heart of his redemptive mission. Their assimilation of Christ as the norm of the spiritual moral life is more than a mere external process of imitation, but an inner communion of the spirits of the believers with the Spirit of Christ himself. This dynamic, inner communion enables Paul to proclaim the death of the old self and the putting on of the new: ". . . the life I live now is not my own; Christ is living in me" (Gal 2:20). It is effected by means of their cooperation with the Spirit of God, an essential element of which is dedicated devotion to the life of prayer.[15]

Jesus and the Moral Imagination

Up until this point little has been said about practical ways Christians can cooperate with Spirit so that their lives truly reflect the person of Jesus as their absolute spiritual moral norm. If, as one eminent New Testament scholar maintains, "one cannot speak of Jesus as the source of a unique ethical system as one can in the case of Aristotle or Kant,"[16] the question still remains to what extent do the Gospel stories actually mediate the universal normative vision of Jesus. This question is compounded by the variety of Christologies presented by the evangelists and, except until relatively recently in the history of moral theology, the merely peripheral relevance of Jesus to disciplined moral reflection in the Church.

One response to this dilemma comes from William Spohn who, like Rigali and Balthasar, maintains that Jesus represents the "concrete universal" of Christian ethics. In his mind:

> [i]f Christians are disciples of Jesus, that implies that his life and teachings are *normative* for them. This relation necessarily means that the disciple acknowledges the authority of the master, particularly when the master lives up to the message. The particular life and death of Jesus set the boundaries for Christians, direct their intentions, and shape the emotions and actions of individuals and communities. That is to say, the life of Jesus functions as their "norm" or standard. Usually we think of moral norms as general statements, such as "equals should be treated equally." The norm for Christian life is more complex and more concrete than that.[17]

---

[15] For a treatment of prayer as communion, see Fabio Giardini, *Pray without Ceasing: Toward a Systematic Psychotheology of Christian Prayerlife* (Rome: Millennium/Gracewing, 1998) 239–78.

[16] Pheme Perkins, "Jesus and Ethics," *Theology Today* 52 (1995) 50.

[17] William C. Spohn, *Go and Do Likewise: Jesus and Ethics* (New York: Continuum, 1999) 10.

Spohn combines three avenues of reflection to help his readers gain access to the normative content of the Gospels: "(a) the New Testament story of Jesus, (b) the ethics of virtue and character, and (c) the practices of Christian spirituality."[18] This threefold methodology helps him to steer clear of those interpretations which ignore Jesus' relationship to Christian ethics altogether either because of the plurality of depictions of Jesus in the New Testament or because of the lack of distinguishing content in his moral teachings. Through the interplay of these approaches, he finds in the analogical imagination the hermeneutical link between Scripture and contemporary ethical practice:

> Jesus did not come teaching timeless moral truths or a uniform way of life to be replicated in every generation. Rather his words, his encounters, and life story set patterns that can be flexibly but faithfully extended to new circumstances. These patterns lead us to envision analogous ways of acting that are partly the same and partly different. As disciples become more conformed to Christ, their imagination spots these patterns and carries them creatively into new realizations.[19]

For Spohn, Jesus' counsel at the end of the parable of the Good Samaritan to "go and do likewise" (Luke 10:37) is the guiding metaphor for Christians as they seek "to put on the mind of Christ" in the circumstances of their daily lives.[20] To do so, Christians must be aware of the basic analogy that guides Christian moral reflection on Scripture: The New Testament is to its world as Christian community is to its world.[21] That means being immersed in the gospel stories themselves, finding appropriate parallels in their own lives, and being aware of possible defective perceptions that might get in the way. It also means dedication to regular practices that shape the lives of believers, especially those of baptism, Eucharist, intercessory prayer, biblical meditation and discernment, forgiveness and solidarity.[22] Through such practices Christians have traditionally been able to ground their moral lives in the person of Jesus Christ. They also provide a unifying context within which such disciplines as spirituality and moral theology and such topics as prayer and conscience can be seen to interact at profound levels.

---

[18] Spohn, *Go and Do Likewise*, 12.

[19] Spohn, *Go and Do Likewise*, 49. For the way in which Jesus renews the moral imagination, see Perkins, "Jesus and Ethics," 51–54.

[20] Spohn, *Go and Do Likewise*, 4, 50.

[21] Spohn, *Go and Do Likewise*, 55.

[22] Spohn, *Go and Do Likewise*, 186.

Listening to the Full Body of Christ

We are now at a point where we can outline in summary fashion some of the skills involved in the "rapt listening" mentioned in some of our earlier chapters. What follows presupposes all that has gone before. The "rapt listener" to the full body of Christ recognizes Christ as the absolute norm of history and the "concrete universal" of the Christian spiritual moral life. This person searches the Scripture with an open heart and employs the analogical imagination to find appropriate applications to the circumstances of his or her life. This person also recognizes and takes into account in his or her spiritual moral discernment the various ecclesial dimensions of Christ's body (i.e., considering the Church as sacrament, mystical communion, institution, herald, and servant). This person also employs a regular regimen of spiritual practices that keeps him or her in touch with Christ and his body, the Church, and which guides his or her moral reflection on the concrete problems of daily life. First and foremost, this person is a man or woman of prayer, someone who takes seriously the Apostle's enjoinder "to pray without ceasing" (1 Thess 5:17) and who seeks to enter into dialogue with Christ and his Church in as intimate a way as possible.

The work of Fabio Giardini on the nature and meaning of unceasing prayer is particularly useful in helping us to draw out some of activities involved in the kind of "rapt listening" we are talking about. Prayer is a dialogue between the human and the divine. As such, it is fundamentally a participatory action: we "share" or "participate in" a conversation with the divine—and vice versa. This dialogue takes place on every anthropological level of human existence: the physical, the emotional, the intellectual, the spiritual, and the social. What is more, it involves an important interplay between "the activity of the mind" and "the activity of the heart" (or "will"), which Giardini refers to respectively as "attention" and "intention."[23] The different types of attention and intention provide us with an apt metaphor for the various dimensions of listening involved in spiritual moral decision-making. Attention can be active, receptive, or ecstatic:

- *active* attention is the mind's focusing on and thinking of God: the proper *human* way of paying discursive attention to God;

- *receptive* attention is the mind's opening up, waiting on and for, silent listening to God: a somewhat *superhuman* way of paying intuitive attention to God;

[23] Giardini, *Pray Without Ceasing*, 39.

- *ecstatic* attention is the mind's total self-forgetful absorption into God's Mystery: an entirely *transhuman* surrender of the whole human mind to God.[24]

These three kinds of attention in prayer parallel the successive stages of interpersonal communication and union. That is to say, "an interpersonal relationship gradually progresses from the mutual speaking/listening stage toward a so silent union of partners that they do not need to talk at all."[25]

As far as the various types of intention are concerned, the nomenclature is generally the same, but the ordering slightly different. This process:

- Begins with the grateful acceptance of God's beneficent love, i.e., with a receptive love-intention.

- Develops by loving God for God's sake, i.e., through an active love-intention.

- Reaches loving oneself for God's sake, i.e., entirely forgetting and surrendering oneself to God by an ecstatic love-intention.[26]

These three kinds of intention fuse into the relationship of being-in-love with God. As a process, it is repeated again and again in a person's life to give him or her a more profound participation in the intimate life of the Trinity. This profound participation eventually seeps down into the person's subliminal consciousness and manifests itself in an attitude of prayerfulness that is brought to all of his or her daily activities.

Giardini later points out that "loving and knowing are both equally essential to the life of prayer and always intertwined within it, although in different proportions and fashions."[27] As such, it makes little sense to engage in a heated debate over which has priority over the other—and in what manner. The whole person enters into the sacred dialogue that is prayer, not a particular faculty or dimension of that person. In Giardini's understanding of unceasing prayer, attention and intention ultimately penetrate the whole person—body, soul, and spirit—in prayer and enable him or her to ascend to God, to address God, to worship God, and to live in communion with Him.

Clearly Giardini's understanding of the various kinds of attention and intention can be applied in analogous fashion to Christ's body, the

---

[24] Giardini, *Pray Without Ceasing*, 55–56.
[25] Giardini, *Pray Without Ceasing*, 57.
[26] Giardini, *Pray Without Ceasing*, 102.
[27] Giardini, *Pray Without Ceasing*, 121.

Church. The believer is called to live in relationship with Christ in and through the mystery of his body. This relationship needs to be nurtured from the earliest moments in a person's life. It means attending to it through active listening to its teaching, a receptive (though not uncritical) response to its demands, and an intellectual union with its inner being and mission. It also means being-in-love with the Church through the reception of Christ's words and actions (at the liturgy), through an active participation in its life (by the dedicated living out of one's vocation), and through a loving union with its universal salvific mission (through a deep sense of identity with Christ and his body). Knowing and loving the Church go hand in hand. As noted in chapter four, to separate them can easily lead a person to the subtle compromises of rationalism and fideism. Each of these does damage to the faith, either by stripping it of its mystery (as in the case of rationalism) or by denying its credibility (as in the case of fideism). What is more, they do damage to the inner unity of the faith by reducing its intrinsic harmony to satisfy only one of the anthropological dimensions of human existence. When seen in this light, Catholics are called not only "to think with the Church," but also "to love with the Church." As members of Christ's body, they use both their minds and their hearts in a "dialogue of communion" that shapes their consciences and aids them in difficult moments of decision.

Practical Implications

Jesus is the norm of morality and his presence pervades the conscience of the believer teaching truth and moving the disciple to make moral judgments in line with that truth. At the heart of conscience then is a conversation between the believer and God in the context of the Christian community. The judgment of conscience is always and everywhere subjectively normative. But how does understanding the conscience as prayerful relate to objective norms? How does it better help one to make that judgment and see the moral truth? Romano Guardini asked:

> If Christ is the category of Christian thought, in what way is the content of this thought given? [This question] is extraordinarily difficult and it appears that theological thought has not as yet taken [it] into consideration. It seems as though it wanted to assure the scientific character of its work by carrying it out according to the philosophical or historical disciplines that build on abstract categories. They see the specific character of Christianity as only consisting in its content, namely, in the authoritative nature of revelation. But as to how Christian conscience, how the Christian

act of knowing and its methodological process, which therefore is
Christian science, ought to be shaped from the fact that Christ is
the category of this conscience and of this knowledge, does not
seem to be an object of theoretical research. It is rather something
to be left to mere devotion to Christ.[28]

Characterizing "devotion" as "mere" highlights what we have been
meditating upon throughout this book: Christ is at the center of moral
thought and judgment not simply an appendage or ornament to be
added on. But surely Christ will be left to "mere devotion" if we cannot
give some examples of how accepting the judgment of conscience as
prayerful furthers Catholic moral living.

Would there be any real effect to the decision-making process if one
was cognizant of Christ being the Voice listened to in the judgment of
conscience and that that listening was a prayer? How might this faith
stance color ethical formation and deliberation, content, and judgment?

A. Process of Formation and Deliberation

The process of becoming one who "prays unceasingly" as we noted
above is the goal of any Christian moral formation. Becoming one who
prays unceasingly in a community that does likewise is itself the work
of ecclesial formation. This kind of formation falls to the local parish
primarily because we are not thinking here of only imparting this
awareness of prayer and conscience to an academic elite. In fact when
discussions about prayer and conscience are raised in pastoral educa-
tional settings very rarely do participants find it an unusual pairing of
theological realities. We can come to an awareness that to judge moral
behavior out of a praying conscience is simply the reconfiguring of
the spiritual principle of practicing the presence of God. There is no
artificial separation between person as believer and person as moral
decision-maker.

The believer thinks out of a different context than the non-believer
and thus his or her conscience formation is accomplished in the arena
of the full body of Christ as noted above. Anything less than this may
reveal a bias or unreflective preference for conclusions already appropriated at other times and perhaps for other than faith reasons. If one
accepts the conscience as a place of prayer then his or her formation

---

[28] Romano Guardini, "The Essence of Christianity," ms., trans. Donald Nesti, Pontifical College Josephinum, Columbus, Ohio.

will always be explicitly ecclesial. By saying this we are recognizing the Church as the sacrament of Christ. Through the Church the presence of Christ is mediated to us and more clearly apprehended. In the complex experience of forming the conscience no person who prays his moral judgments can call those judgments explicitly Christian without a deep attachment to ecclesial sources of moral truth. Being embedded in the tradition and community is a way to test the "voices" in our minds and come to see which one or ones carry truth. Michael Casey says, "Those who are transformed by prayer, instead of becoming spectacular mystics, become humble human beings."[29] It is this humility, the disposition to act upon and live the truth that truly characterizes the fruit of prayer-filled ethics. What is novel about this humility, however, is that it is the fruit of communication with God from within the Church and not simply the self-enclosed mind making a decision.

> I do not say that its [conscience] particular injunctions are always clear, or that they are always consistent with each other; but what I am insisting on here is this, that it *commands*. . . . It is more than a man's own self. . . .
>
> Its very existence throws us out of ourselves and beyond ourselves, to go and seek for Him in the height and depth, whose voice it is.[30]

Further, Mark O'Keefe argues that practicing a prayerful life disposes a person to more easily hear and recognize the divine voice at the moment of moral judgment.[31]

And so in the formation of conscience the unique characteristic of the prayer-imbued conscience is that the person desires to spend time at the sources of encounter with Christ, be they the Word of God or embedded in the Sacraments. The conscience is also directly affected by one's service to the poor to the extent that the person is open to see Christ in all who are needy. The deliberation of one who is cognizant of the judgment of a prayerful conscience will be open and receptive to spiritual direction as he or she searches for moral truth. He or she will not simply accept what is current in culture or popular in political ideology but will seek out those in the Christian community who have attempted to transcend bias and live in open conversation with deeper

[29] Michael Casey, *Toward God: The Ancient Wisdom of Western Prayer* (Liguori, Mo.: Triumph Books, 1989) 144.

[30] John Henry Newman, *Sermons Preached on Various Occasions* (London: Longmans, Green, & Co., 1900) 64–65.

[31] Mark O'Keefe, *Becoming Good, Becoming Holy: On the Relationship of Christian Ethics and Spirituality* (Mahwah, N.J.: Paulist Press, 1995) 121.

currents of human meaning. The move to converse with a "spiritual" mentor and not simply seek out one knowledgeable in social science, politics or psychotherapy marks a real conversion in the person who apprehends the spiritual depths of moral deliberation. As Vincent McNamara said so rightly, "Moral discernment has to be done in fidelity to who one is as a Christian. One must do full justice to the moral agent."[32] The ethic of Christianity carries with it a personal call, not simply a duty to be responsible or thoughtful. Christian moral discernment occurs within one's personal disposition to be open to the Christ. In this openness, both the personal love one has for God in Christ and the intellect's grasp of what is morally true coalesce; thus in discipleship we take on the mind of Christ.

B. The Content of Moral Behavior

In light of this formation, would the content of Christian moral behavior lend itself to a unique fashioning? Probably not. That is to say that this prayerful ethic would be no more or no less than the Christian ethic. It is this ethic that is based on faith and reason discerning moral value for a particular question, or forming a particular virtue. However, the moral behavior of a person who is aware of the prayerfulness of his conscience would carry the distinctive mark of gratitude and/or worship before and after the actual apprehension of truth and judgment.

C. The Actual Judgment

In the actual judgment of conscience the Christian will come to believe that in his or her best effort to ascertain the truth, God's voice has been heard. In this faith stance regarding moral judgment the person specifies and names his or her conversation partner in the quest for moral truth. One has not entered an "insurmountable solitude" in the conscience. One has not closed the door upon the self, but rather one has opened the door of the mind and welcomed its creator—God. In the deliberations and judgments of the praying person moral knowledge is *not to be grasped* at through "curiosity" or through an avarice for knowledge, *but is received*. This reality of receiving wisdom reflects the stance of humility before truth, a stance that is not without personal

---

[32] Vincent McNamara, *Faith and Ethics: Recent Roman Catholicism* (Washington, D.C.: Georgetown University Press, 1985) 204.

engagement, but emphasizes docility more than autonomy. Since all judgments of conscience are personal (I can never make one for you) we learn what is good *not only* by listening to God in the conscience but by following through on what we have heard in action. St. Bonaventure notes: "A man becomes wise not merely by listening: he must also conform. . . . A sick man is not healed by listening to a physician: he must also follow his prescription."[33] Bonaventure has a perspective on knowledge that he calls the science of the saints. It is a knowledge that leads to action out of love for truth.[34] And in the end this is what is most characteristic of a prayer-imbued ethic. It is an approach to making moral decisions that actively seeks to listen to the wisdom of God because the person making the moral judgments *loves* that wisdom. This approach is not simply interested in getting the right answer. Rather, one is interested in getting the right answer to moral questions in the context of loving the One who is always and everywhere *breathing* the right answer into the human spirit.

This breathing, of course, is not a replacement for thinking but the very fulfillment of all that the one who loves truth desires. In other words our search for the morally true and good is met by the living God from within our spirit and therefore directed and completed by God. This is why Christ is the moral norm. Human reason in its openness to truth never fully reaches completion. Faith is not a constraint upon reason or truth but is its completion. At the depth of conscience is not autonomous reason but reason's completion in truth, the truth which is a *person*, Christ.[35] All that was human the living God took on in Christ, and because of that "taking on," we hope in a God who now fills our very humanity with his divine presence, elevating us to share in the divine truth through healed human realities.

What prayer as the context for ethical decision-making really highlights is the paradoxical openness and limitation that belief in God invites us to and places upon us. At a time when scientists are claiming to be able to find the material somatic and chemical causes of formerly "moral" problems, (excessive drinking, anger, homosexuality, adultery, etc.) the presence of God in ethics cannot be taken for granted. In this age all is reduced to matter and controlled by chemicals. How can God's voice be heard or even thought to exist in a day when we label

[33] Bonaventure, St., *Collationes in Hexameron et Bonaventuriana quaedam selecta,* ed. F. M. Delorme (Quaracchi: Collegium S. Bonaventurae, 1934) 2:3 (V, 337a), as quoted in Charles Carpenter, *Theology as the Road to Holiness in St. Bonaventure* (Mahwah, N.J.: Paulist Press, 1999) 149.

[34] Carpenter, *Theology as the Road to Holiness,* 160.

[35] See Joseph Ratzinger, "Conscience and Truth," *Crisis of Conscience,* ed. John Haas (New York: Crossroad Publishing, 1996) 1–20.

the "formally" immoral as now simply the genetically directed or chemically unbalanced? As of yet few claim that chemical and genetic realities *fully determine* behavior in all cases but simply that these exercise a powerful influence over the body and its desires. Is there still a secret "sanctuary" left within the human heart to which one can "go" to listen to God? Has conscience and its judgment of truth been replaced by drugs, mind by matter?[36]

It is valid to believe in a God who creates matter and then wills this matter to grow and develop in accord with its own makeup of certain chemicals and cells and more basic molecular building blocks. But is it necessary or even real to invite this God, in this kind of creation, to be involved in a quest for moral truth? If mind is reduced to matter, we can worship God as creator but not as good in the moral sense; in the sense that one's mind detects what is good for the human and moves away from what is against his or her dignity. In our current world there is simply the secular, the material, the facts or information. Human spirit is retreating and so therefore is the self in relation to God. More than ever an exploration into the human capacity to pray and to actually have that prayer yield wisdom about human behavior is crucial for sustaining a vision of life beyond the material and secular. This is not to deny that many behaviors formally thought of as simply moral, as simply reasoned, willed and chosen, have some etiology in body chemistry. How then shall we relate prayer and conscience to these influential material causes of behavior? Basically we approach them through a renewed meditation upon the incarnation and all that such a belief means regarding the worth of our embodiedness. There is an obsessive grasping for control in the secular way of thinking, which wants to take, look at, name, and master all. We are less likely to want to listen to where our controlling desires *have* taken us or *are* taking us now in society. We are afraid that listening to God will limit us. It will unmask our real disposition at times, "I am not God and *that* is not good." And after our controlling and discovering of all that moves us and pushes us and paradoxically just as relentlessly decays, what then? Does the soul have bodily connections? Do we quiet the soul, the doorway to God, by our urgent actions to name and control reality? Moral living is inherently embodied as all that we become presents itself publicly through our bodily self. But that which is bodily and material is not the only reality. Through and within the material world the Holy Spirit speaks and calls to us to yield to wisdom.

---

[36] See Robert Coles, *The Secular Mind* (Princeton, N.J.: Princeton University Press, 1999) 178.

The self that is in relation to God is not simply "matter become conscious of itself," but matter that becomes conscious of self as related to God. In this identity one is also given a mission. Self consciousness is only the beginning, the deeper listening to God through the conscience expands one's identity to engage in mission. We are literally "sent" to do the good by conscience, which mediates the voice of God. In this way the person *serves* the moral truth and is not simply impelled to do this or that by genetic or chemical influence.[37] The self in relation to others and God is always reaching out for communion with its authentic end in such relations. It is this reaching out or down toward what is "most real" about the human identity that characterizes the work of conscience as a listening for God. In light of the threat to human dignity in materialist, political, cultural or economic reductionism, the person, in the context of the communion of saints, receives the presence of God through faith, hope and love and clings to this way of living. The triumph of the person over the forces of reductionism is best expressed in the approach to freedom founded upon commitment to the moral good in prayer.

Practically speaking prayer is not to be "used" to get right moral answers. There is a "utilitarian" aspect to intercessory prayer, but the prayer of the conscience is simply the stance of one who wishes to order his or her world according to the meaning of being in the presence of Holiness itself. As a *fruit* of attending to this presence and approaching the search for moral goodness in deference to divine wisdom one receives the truth about the self and therefore a direction is given regarding the nature of one's dispositions and behavior. Prayer does not exhaust the moral formation project, but it does ground it and give it a secure position amid reductionist trends and the passing cultural and political fads that clamor to define us. Emphasizing prayer can thus dull the secularization of the current age and give an authentic religious reality to moral inquiry. Upon what secular pool of moral formation, for example, will we draw when moral truth asks for the death of selfishness?[38] Our faith has a rich theological expertise in dying and death, in renouncing and "giving up" what is simply sufficient but not complete. Prayer, the expression of faith in God, can equip us to yield over the ego and selfishness in "death." This referencing of death, of course, bespeaks the entire moral project in light of the Paschal Mystery. Christians in their entire moral-spiritual life enter the prayer of Jesus to the Father upon the cross and receive the ability

---

[37] Hans Urs von Balthasar, *Mysterium Paschale* (Edinburgh: T. & T. Clark, 1990) 91f.

[38] Alasdair C. MacIntyre, *Secularization and Moral Change* (London: Oxford University Press, 1967).

through grace to live the good life "through the power of the resurrection." (Phil 3:10)[39]

Beyond Moral Methodology

Whether Catholics assent to all moral doctrine or question them or even actually dissent in their action *against* Catholic moral doctrine, pastoral leadership is still obliged to *teach the doctrine* in the context of prayer and moral discernment. Built upon a virtue ethic the prayer-imbued conscience can be understood to personally appropriate truths already defined by the Church's magisterium or, more dramatically, it can be shown a truth not yet defined. In this process of coming to truth within a tradition,[40] that necessarily has to be ordered by an authority, we are to be alert for two temptations: blind obedience,[41] as opposed to legitimate trust in God toward things not fully seen, and secondly, individualism and pride. Ultimately, because moral truth orders the common good, even the dissenting "prophetic" parishioner or theologian has to have the content of their dissent recognized as the truth and

---

[39] Brian Johnstone, "Resurrection and Moral Theology" *Josephinum Journal of Theology* 7:1-2 (Summer 2000) 5–17.

[40] Brian Johnstone has noted a helpful distinction when trying to understand the role of tradition in moral formation. He identifies two realities in this question, the tradition of truth and the tradition of identity. In the tradition of truth one discovers an *objective* coherence , and a source of coherence *within the self* from a tradition's beliefs and norms. This coherence enables one to move beyond interior conflicts and pursue the good originally sought in the tradition in an integrated manner. There cannot be an ethics outside and above all tradition. A tradition must be able to promise a transcendent good that goes beyond the mere preservation of identity. Tradition of identity is when the preservation of identity is the preeminent good, blinding the participants to the fact that some aspects of their living may not be in coherence with valued moral goods. Identity is a good, but *as a condition* for seeking a good which *transcends group identity*. In this confused tradition the moral good *is* only the preservation of the group's known identity as it exists in the current political and cultural and historical epoch. Brian Johnstone, "Can Tradition Be A Source of Moral Truth? A Reply to K.W. Merks," *Studia Moralia* 37:2 (1999) 441–47.

[41] If one understands "blind obedience" as an act of trust in the truth the Spirit brings, then certainly there is a place for such a trust in the moral life. For example, it is certainly an act of trust to obey the imperative of conscience as it speaks a truth of change to the person. In the early stages of relinquishing a vice and taking up a virtue, quite often we proceed "blindly," not having the old securities of habit and familiar responses to situations. We trust profoundly in God and go forward in "darkness." This appears legitimate. Blind obedience in a more narrow sense, construed as a response to an authoritarian construct at the cost of one's own appropriation of moral truth, appears more as "power over" than truth discovered. This is to be rejected. See *Veritatis Splendor* 42 and *Guadium et Spes* 17.

defined as such by the teaching authority of the Church. In fact, that is what most "dissenters" hope will happen; to see an appropriation of the truth they "discovered" come to be defined by the magisterium as a legitimate development of doctrine. Their personal crisis begins when the vision they apprehended in discernment and prayer is not defined by the magisterium as such. How will envisioning prayer at the core of conscience impact these two pastoral situations; the faithful parishioner appropriating defined moral doctrine and the dissenting parishioner hoping to witness to an as yet defined doctrine?

First, as we briefly stated above, we think that prayer in the context of conscience can purify the influence of secularistic or simply current ideologies. It may assist in discerning, therefore, the difference between "weeds and wheat" in the moral and political talk of popular culture. How does it do this? Prayer in the context of conscience is the essence of *sacrum commercium*, it is a sacred exchange which relativizes all other exchanges be they political or economic. In its basic "turn to the other" conscience in the context of prayer re-establishes the priority of relatedness to God as fundamental to knowing and doing the moral truth. In this knowing of the truth in a sacred exchange the person will have to suffer the reception of the truth due to previous habits of viciousness not yet purified. In seeing the judgment of conscience in the context of prayer one can gain the strength to do the truth despite this suffering. In this "doing," one's memory of the presence of God in prayerful moral judgment will initiate a habit of progressive ease in listening for the truth in future moral imperatives.[42]

This exchange does not, however, cut the disciple off from sources of truth outside of explicit faith. The conscience receives the truth from secular sources as well but it does not give those *sources* ultimacy, only the *truth* is given ultimacy. Moreover being a person of prayer does not necessarily give a person immediate and correct answers to ethical questions per se. One can pray and still be wrong in moral judgment. The alternative is true as well; one can make a true moral judgment and never open the heart in prayer.[43] (It is not at all clear as to whether a person can be hostile and against prayer and still be virtuous, while lacking such piety.). These qualifications simply point out the limited

---

[42] See Johann Baptist Metz, *A Passion for God*, trans. J. Matthew Ashley (Mahwah, N.J.: Paulist Press, 1998) 143–49.

[43] We are here simply acknowledging that not every person is a Christian and that authentic moral judgments can be made by non believers. For the believer it appears morally questionable to intentionally ignore, deny or leave un-integrated the moral and spiritual life. Brian V. Johnstone, "The Dynamics of Conversion," *Spirituality and Morality*, ed. Dennis Billy and Donna Orsuto (Mahwah, N.J.: Paulist, 1996) 45–47.

and finite nature of all that is human. These qualifications do not stand as an argument for the *intentional separation* of ethics and spirituality. In fact, one could argue that for the disciple of Christ the possibility of knowing the good without prayer and conversely engaging in prayer that does not open the self to the moral truth is a living invitation to better integrate these two.

In this work of integration a state of faithful discipleship is created despite finitude and lack. In the end the question of prayer and its relation to conscience is one about the reality of being faithful to Christ in the midst of Christian community; a community that participates in the mysteries of faith unto public moral witness. Acknowledging our limits and even our sinfulness only presses us further on to cooperate with grace in the work of fidelity to such an identity. Failing to discern the objective moral truth on occasion, even as a person of prayer, is no cause for neurotic guilt or flights into perfectionist *Angst*. It is simply a summons to move us toward the continual reception of the mercy of God and the psychological and spiritual rest that is afforded us there.

Conclusion

Thus, the member of the church who disagrees with defined doctrine needs to see, for example, if his or her conscience is heavily influenced by politically liberal or conservative ideology. The faithful parishioner needs to see if his or her appropriation of the moral doctrine is really *personal*. It is not a matter of saying that prayerful persons will never find difficulty with doctrine so defined or that these *faithful* ones will be able to articulate and live fully the truth. The key, the commonality for both types of parishioners is the response in grace to God's invitation to become united to him in truth. In faith their prayers will be answered and eventually one will be shown his or her *objective* error. *Subjectively* he or she will have been graced as one who *seeks* the truth. The other person, conversely, may be *objectively* correct but subjectively separated from the truth that he or she never fully appropriated as real, as his or her own. Of course there are those who see clearly or hear correctly and are congruent in both their apprehension of truth and their personal appropriation of it. It is to them and their methods of discernment and prayer that we turn for guidance.

William Spohn notes:

> Perceiving God's action requires a willingness to be affected by what one sees, an initial disposition to respond favorably to what is good and true. The good news is inviting to those who have ears

to hear (Mt 19:12). It sounds threatening to those who are closed. "Having ears to hear," that is, a readiness to perceive, is a precondition for correct interpretation. Without that openness many of the most knowledgeable guardians of Israel's traditions missed the message that was the culmination of their history (the coming of the reign of God in their time). Their intellectual preparation did not make them open to healing and transformation.[44]

In a prayerfully disposed conscience, we can attain what Spohn is describing here. Intellectual preparation is good only as far as it goes. We are more than minds in our search and execution of what is good and true. We are vulnerable listeners waiting to be affected by what our God has come to say. If we do not welcome the Christ, and his powerful words of truth and his witness unto death out of love for the Father and for ourselves, we are simply left with posturing and political power, factions, cohorts and special interest groups. These realities cannot bear the weight of forming Christian disciples. This kind of formation can only be faithfully undergone in Christian community nourishing itself on "faith and morals," prayer and *doxa*.

---

[44] Spohn, *Go and Do Likewise*, 83.

Conclusion

Still, how hopeful is a purely reasonable approach to such complex issues as abortion and environmental pollution? Self-interest is pervasive. If the best that Christians can offer is to be more reasonable, then the churches might as well retire from the field [of ethics] and stop cluttering an already cluttered moral landscape.[1]

This book on prayer and Christian conscience is an effort to accent what is characteristic of Christian ethical decision-making and so promote a vision that does not simply "clutter" the moral landscape. There are certainly other features of Christian conscience that distinguish it besides its relationship to prayer, but we can think of none so basic.

In bringing morality and prayer together in conscience, we united a universal (i.e., reason) with a particular (i.e., faith, prayer). Rahner's understanding of transcendent activity (love, freedom, thinking) assists a person in understanding how such a union can reasonably occur in light of Christian faith. As for believers, the union is not so difficult, per se. However, there is a dangerous temptation from the vice of intellectual sloth to reduce the prayerful conscience to illuminism and/or positivism. It was our aim to articulate a place for prayer in Christian ethics, so as to help to uproot such a vice and criticize another tendency in moral theology of late, rationalism, in the solving of moral dilemmas.

Some of these rationalistic leanings have laudatory roots in the thinking of scholars who were fascinated with secularity. We have benefited greatly from their probings in this area.

Generally, their thinking brings a deeper awareness of what the Incarnation of God truly means. In saying this, we are simply noticing how focusing upon reason can help believers appreciate the secular, the human, in its own right. However, we believe that this turn toward

[1] B. Waters and R. Stuart, "Being Good and Being Reasonable," *Theology Today* 5 (October 1993) 358.

the secular has muted other important characteristics of moral theology: the holy, devotion, and love.

Finally, this book has been an effort to accomplish what Kenneth Himes once called for: "What is needed is a middle way which does not separate human reasoning processes from the guidance of the Spirit yet does not simply identify the two realities."[2] By utilizing the reality of conscience in moral judgment, and adhering to an understanding of its role as echoing the divine voice, we propose a middle way between a Christian ethics reduced to rationalism and one that is simply sentimental devotionalism. Our understanding of Karl Rahner's existential ethic best summarizes what we believe is accomplished in uniting prayer and moral decision-making in the conscience: conscience grasps what has to be done by me individually and integrates the love of God with the search for truth.[3]

---

[2] Kenneth Himes, "The Contribution of Theology to Catholic Moral Theology," *Moral Theology: Challenges for the Future*, ed. Curran, 60.

[3] Rahner, *Theological Investigations* 2:229.

Index of Names